Annotated Legal Documents on Islam in Europe: Denmark

Annotated Legal Documents on Islam in Europe

VOLUME 18

The titles published in this series are listed at *brill.com/ldie*

Annotated Legal Documents on Islam in Europe

Denmark

Compiled, Annotated and Authored by

Niels Valdemar Vinding

BRILL

LEIDEN | BOSTON

Library of Congress Cataloging-in-Publication Data

Names: Vinding, Niels Valdemar, compiler.
Title: Annotated legal documents on Islam in Europe. Denmark / compiled, annotated and authored by Niels Valdemar Vinding.
Description: Boston : Brill, 2020. | Series: Annotated legal documents on Islam in Europe, 2214-1340 ; 18 | Includes bibliographical references and index. | In English and Danish.
Identifiers: LCCN 2020027143 | ISBN 9789004434943 (paperback) Subjects: LCSH: Muslims–Legal status, laws, etc.–Denmark.
Classification: LCC KJR2467.M56 V56 2020 | DDC 342.48908/5297–dc23
LC record available at https://lccn.loc.gov/2020027143

Typeface for the Latin, Greek, and Cyrillic scripts: "Brill". See and download: brill.com/brill-typeface.

ISSN 2214-1340
ISBN 978-90-04-43494-3 (paperback)

This book is printed on acid-free paper and produced in a sustainable manner.

Contents

Foreword by the Editors

This is the eighteenth volume in the series *Annotated Legal Documents on Islam in Europe*. The publication of this series responds to the widespread lack of sound information about the legal status of Islam in Europe. In principle, this information is easily available to those who are willing to make the effort and know enough about the subject to ask the right questions of the digital search engines. But that requires both expertise and effort, and it takes place in an environment where the public political debate on Islam in many European countries is characterised by increasing concern and fear. Islam has come to be broadly perceived as a security issue rather than a religion like others in Europe. But the concern has also moved into the legal field, most markedly, of course, with discussions about limitations on Muslim female dress enacted in a growing number of countries, or the ban on building minarets on mosques in Switzerland, or restrictions on building mosques in certain Austrian provinces. At the same time, in a number of European states like Austria and Germany, legislation is enacted and state treaties are negotiated which aim to establish a stable and reliable basis for Muslim life and organisation. Even so, such measures are under scrutiny by an increasingly sceptical European public, sometimes ignoring the legal principles of secularity, not least the demands of state neutrality towards and equal treatment of all religions and beliefs regardless of numbers of adherents or public reputation.

In addition, the religious status and rights of Muslims in the various European countries differ significantly, due to different historical developments regarding the organisation of the relations between the state and religions. Furthermore, while in some states laws regulating such matters introduced decades ago are still in force and have to be re-interpreted in the face of a 'newcomer' religion, others have introduced new laws that consider the increasing religious plurality within Europe. Despite the common legal and political foundations constructed since 1945 in instruments such as the European Convention on Human Rights and the more recently accumulated legislation of the European Union, this closer look reveals remarkable differences due to the extent of separating state and religion or establishing co-operative structures. In some countries Islam has an officially recognised status which in some cases originated in the first half of the 20th century. In other countries, no such recognition of any religion is available even if informal ways of favouring one religion over another may exist. Since 1990 especially, European courts have moved to equalise the status of Islam with that of other religions in the practical exercise of religious freedom in various countries. Particular practices regarded as core religious obligations—in the case of Muslims dress codes and practices such as male circumcision, access to correctly slaughtered meat and otherwise *halal* food, free time for the main periods of worship and religious festivals, and the right to build mosques—can be controversial in some countries while less so in others. In the course of the ongoing process of self-organisation and the participation of Muslims in civil societies and their co-operation with the state, children's access to Islamic religious instruction or the education of Muslim theologians can be achieved in co-operation with the state education systems in some countries, while in others the community must rely on its own arrangements. The practically pressing issue of financing the religious infrastructure is still far from being settled in many countries.

The aim of this series is to make this legislation available to both the interested researcher and the practising lawyer. Altogether the series is expected to comprise 32 volumes, one for each of the 27 countries of the European Union plus the United Kingdom, Norway and Switzerland, and a volume each dealing with the European Union (treaties, directives and decisions of the Court of Justice of the European Communities) and the European Court of Human Rights. Excerpts of relevant legislation are introduced and summarised by the volume compiler, and where court cases have provided significant interpretation of the law they will also be referred to. The legislation itself is reproduced in the original language, as the editors and the publisher agreed early on in the preparation of the series that any attempt to translate legislation into English would be unsatisfactory and risked being misleading. The comments and amalysis by the author should give sufficient guidance to users to allow a decision as to whether to arrange a translation for their specific purposes.

While there is in many countries legislation explicitly referring to aspects of Islam, most often regarding official recognition or to do with education, in other countries there is none. Denmark is one of those countries where Islam and Muslims have frequently and for some time been at the centre of public political and media discourse. This is reflected in legislative developments in recent years. The situation is further complicated by the central role of the Evangelical-Lutheran Church of Denmark (*Folkekirken*) in public administration and national culture. Smaller religious communities, including Islam, have always been able to obtain forms of legal recognition, a system which has recently been reformed.

An attempt has been made to ensure that the volumes are structured in as similar a manner as possible. The starting point for this has been the thematic organisation used variously in the *Yearbook of Muslims in Europe* which Brill has published annually since 2009. But it has been only a starting point, and in each volume the compiler and the editors have agreed on the structure which makes most sense for the legislation of the country concerned. Normally one member of the editorial group takes responsibility for discussing the structure and compilation of each volume with the compiler: in this instance, this task was undertaken by Prof. Jørgen Nielsen. We are also grateful to Kate Elliott for the care shown in copy editing the volume. The initiative for this project came from the publisher, where Nicolette van der Hoek and Nienke Brienen-Moolenaar have played an invaluable role in ensuring that the project has maintained its momentum. As editors, we appreciate how much their expertise contributes to ensuring that a project like this can run smoothly.

It is in the nature of such a project that each volume, if left as it stands, will gradually become out of date as new legislation and cases appear. From 2019 the series has become available online in a format which in due course will permit regular updating.

The Editors
May 2020

General Introduction

Islam and the Muslim community in Denmark should arguably be understood and considered analytically in the particular contexts of Danish state, church, society and national culture. While the importance of considering context may be somewhat self-evident, it is nevertheless decisive to pay close attention to it, because Danish Islamic communities and Muslims as minorities are neither particularly clearly defined nor their impact and influence particularly weighty. This means that other interests and additional defining and influential social forces have considerably more impact.

As will become evident in the pages and chapters to follow, there is no single logic regulating and governing Islam and Muslim communities in Denmark. Rather, two analytical perspectives may be hypothesised and discussed in exploring the empirical evidence of the documents cited. The first of these perspectives considers the general framework and discusses the dichotomy of legitimising and delegitimising trends in the governing model of religion in Denmark. The second considers the specific case of the Islamic communities in their particular contexts and discusses the binary of enabling and disabling trends in current legislation. These perspectives are of course related and are problematised further throughout, but will be highlighted for analytical and conceptual reasons in understanding the regulatory contexts.

A General Framework of the Danish Model of Regulating Religion

The first analytical perspective considers the general regulatory paradigm of religion in Denmark. Here, of course, the Church of Denmark is of great importance and much public discourse and legislation concern this particular institution. However, considering religion generally, constitutionally and legally two different sentiments are expressed. First, there is a general appreciation in the normative framework for religion in Denmark. This concerns the predominant place of the Church of Denmark in the constitution, which in Article 4 expresses the idea that the Church should be supported as such. Also, in accordance with Article 6, the head of state must be a member of the Church. In addition, freedom of religion and a considerable degree of autonomy are allowed for religious communities. In light of recent legislation, particularly the *Act on Religious Communities outside the Church of Denmark,* Danish scholars conclude that a "first, important step has been taken towards a new regulation of the relationship between state and religion" (Lemann Kristiansen 2019, 116) and that the powers that be "want to support the religious, both inside and outside the Church of Denmark" (Rytter 2019, 90). This is seen as being in line with the governing Danish model of regulating religion, which holds that religion may be seen as an appreciated and legitimate part of public life (Christoffersen 2012, Christoffersen 2019b).

A second sentiment being expressed as part of the general regulatory framework is that religion must indeed be regulated and that its support and autonomy should be limited. Especially in light of recent legislation, which is discussed further in the chapters to come, the current jurisprudence seeks to increase the regulatory prerogative of parliament. A case in point is the recent shift in constitutional thinking on the limits of discrimination, which is evident in ongoing discussions of Article 70. The particular wording of the constitution means that no-one may be deprived of the full enjoyment of civic or political rights by reason of 'his confession,' and here the current argument of the legislature is that the provison forbids discrimination against an individual on the basis of 'his' religion, but allows for general discrimination of religions, as long as it is equitable, proportionate and warranted. Lisbet Christoffesen has criticised this argument (Christoffersen 2019b, 17) and points to an equally worrying trend in a shift in the constitutional theory regarding freedom of religion, set out in Article 67, which allows for free worship, except where it 'contravenes decency or public order.' Usually and in light of international law and human rights law, Article 67 is understood to imply that only law may limit freedom of religion, but in light of discussions of circumcision, it is argued that a certain degree of 'discretion' may be allowed in limiting religion (Christoffersen 2019b, 22–23). Taken together with other limitations of public support for religious activites, as in the amendment to the *Public Education Act* and the explicit demands for decorum and democratic forms and order, there seems to be a trend that seeks to limit or deligitimise the presence of religion in public life, specifically concerning teaching of doctrine and education.[1]

1 On the limits to public and civic participation, see Vinding 2019a, "Civilsamfundet og udgrænsningen af de danske trossamfund", in Brian Arly Jacobsen, Henrik Reintoft Christensen & Signe A.E. Larsen (eds.), *Religion i det offentlige rum—et dansk perspektiv* (Aarhus: Aarhus Universitetsforlag, 2019).

The Specific Case of Islamic Communities in Their Danish Context

The second analytical perspective considers Islam, Islamic religious communities and Muslims as a specific case in the context and relationship with the Church of Denmark, as well as state, society and culture. Here, a binary set of regulatory logics is at work, which at times seems to come into conflict, or at least point in different directions. On the one hand, Islamic communities are to a certain degree enabled by public legislation, most significantly the *Act on Religious Communities outside the Church of Denmark*, but on the other hand, Islamic communities are disabled by much of the recent legislation.

The first of these two logics follows from the legal paradigm of the state's relationship with the Church of Denmark, which is in part problematised in light of a longer secularist discourse that seeks to re-define the nature of this legal paradigm. As the Church of Denmark is by far the most significant and important religious community in Denmark, much of the relations between state and Islam is regulated in the light of this majority church. Rights that the Church of Denmark holds, and which are not in their nature specific to that institution, are by analogy and practice extended to other religious communities, including Islamic communities. The same goes for rights that are seen as general to religious communities, which are often derived from the constitution and aligned with international law on freedom of religion and belief. As is demonstrated across the different areas of law, access to pastoral care and religious services, to marriage and to mediation in divorce and much more is extended due either to the status of the Church of Denmark or to the protections of freedom of religion and belief. As seen from the analytical focus on Islam, this approach may be understood as particularly *enabling* in its regulation of religion and works according to sound principles of law. Further, it appears as if this aspect of regulation of religion is not very politicised. A case in point is discussed in chapter 15.3 on Mediation, where an executive order on ecclesiastical mediation in cases of separation and divorce allows for such mediation also amongst other religious communities. Considering many of the political debates and discussions referred to in what follows, it seems that permission for religious mediation is sanctioned by law.

The second distinct logic comes with the political and public debates on the place of religion in particular, and Islam specifically, that have resurfaced in 21st-century legislation. By contrast this seems to be *disabling* to Islam and Muslim communities in Denmark. At the core is the question of how and where to draw the line between state power and public religion, especially Islam and Muslim communities, and about how much power and influence they each have. In particular, a search for the political and legal basis of religious communities' legitimate contributions to Danish society begins with the observation in legal and political texts that have appeared since the international crisis (the 'cartoons crisis') that followed the publication of the twelve cartoons of Muhammad in *Jyllands-Posten* on 30 September 2005. In the light of the many reactions for and against the publication of those cartoons there seems to be an underlying conflict between the political and legislative power, on the one hand, and public, organised religion, especially the Muslim communities, on the other. The political and legislative changes that followed the cartoons crisis marked both a continuation of an existing political logic and yet something entirely new (Vinding 2019a). In a 2011 analysis of the crisis, Carsten Stage concluded that the crisis was the beginning of something new in Denmark and that the event was central to a shift in the negotiation of national identity (Stage 2011, 185). Stage's analysis considers three competing discourses in what he sees as the Danish struggle following an increased awareness of globalisation. Apart from an altruistic discourse, which emphasises nationality as the ability to value and deal with human and cultural diversity, Stage identifies a 'rationalist discourse' and a so-called 'primordialism discourse.' In both, Islam and Muslims appear to be highly contested. In the discourse of rationalism, Muslims' mixing of religion and politics is particularly criticised as they do not seem to engage with contemporary rationality and reason. In the primordialism discourse, Muslims emerge as actors who are angry with Denmark and want to limit and contest Danish values, which some right-wing voices see as reason to defend Danish cultural institutions, including popular Christianity (Stage 2011, 188–189). Such attitudes are not new, but after the cartoons crisis they appear more clearly articulated and more legitimate than ever before. Common to both these discourses and the particular new aspect is the political will to legislate on the basis that Islam and 'deviant' religion is alien in the public space in Denmark, regardless of any history with deviant Christian denominations, Judaism or other religion. Certain aspects of Islam and 'the way certain Muslims practise' are understood—both politically and legislatively—as a negative influence on society and social cohesion.

The 2016 'Agreement Paper' and the Recent Legislative Agenda

Such binary logics as both legitimising and deligimising public religion and enabling and disabling Islam have been particularly predominant in the recent legislative agenda. The political logic and readiness to delegitimise public religion generally, and to legislate against Islam and Muslims, both directly and indirectly, reached its peak in the months and years after a three-part television documentary entitled 'Mosques behind the Veil', which aired in March 2016. While the documentary did give some insight into teaching and preaching in particular mosques, all worthwhile understanding and nuance in the documentary was sacrificed for the one goal of demonstrating the prevalent extremism. The documentary employed questionable journalistic techniques, including the use of undercover informants and hidden cameras, to expose Danish mosques and imams who are extremist Islamist and Salafist in views and practice. While the factual insight into and nature of the problems are indeed worthwhile to discuss,[2] the documentary in effect gave impetus to a remarkable legislative agenda. Throughout 2016, 2017 and 2018 more than a dozen laws, amendments and executive orders have come into force that not only addressed immigration, asylum seekers and foreigners in Denmark, but also have had a considerable impact on Islam and Muslims in Denmark, as well as on other religious communities. On 31 May 2016, a few months after the airing of the documentary, the Minister of Ecclesiastical Affairs, Bertel Haarder, presented a so-called 'Agreement Paper'[3]—sometimes also referred to as the 'imam package'—outlining a number of specific initiatives to curtail religious preachers who allegedly seek to undermine Danish laws, freedoms and values and support parallel views of law. The eight-page document accompanied by seven appendices constituted an in-principle agreement by the then Liberal Party minority government and the Social Democrats, the Danish People's Party and the Conservatives, collectively representing a substantial majority in parliament. The Agreement Paper states as its purpose to present new initiatives on three themes, namely, withdrawing public recognition of some religious communities, limiting the entry of so-called 'hate preachers', and establishing sanctions to be imposed on individuals and communities that undermine the core values of Danish society.

As will be seen and critically discussed in several instances below, the political will of the legislative programme was to go as far as constitutionally possible to limit religious freedom and Islamist iterations and radical Muslim affairs, specifically, that are perceived as subversive to democracy, counter to equality or arguing for parallel legal orders. And in the individual amendments and bills set out here it is clear that the drafting jurists have sought such limits, not

2 As does, for example, the 'Danish Mosques—Significance, Use and Influence' research project at the University of Copenhagen. https://www.mosques.ku.dk

3 "Aftale mellem regeringen og Socialdemokraterne, Dansk Folkeparti og Det Konservative Folkeparti om initiativer rettet mod religiøse forkyndere, som søger at undergrave danske love og værdier og understøtte parallelle retsopfattelser", Ministry of Ecclesiastical Affairs, doc. no. 65672/16, 31 May 2016. https://www.km.dk/fileadmin/share/kursus/Aftalepapir.pdf, accessed 1 November 2019.

just invoking the criticism of Muslim groups, but also from legal professional organisations, human rights watch institutions, churches and other religious communities. While it must be argued that it is of course the business of public authorities to work for equality, democracy, and rights and freedoms and against subversive institutions and negative impact on social cohesion and public order, it must equally be stressed—as do many of the critical voices—that such efforts must be within the framework of good governance and the rule of law and live up to the criteria of quality of law. Much of the actual legislation has been criticised and some of it does not meet international standards or fails to live up to the legislative ideals of proportionality or necessity. Moreover, some of the law may very well prove difficult to implement, or ineffective, or even just tokenistic. Some of it may even prove to be indirect discrimination and to do more harm than good. This seems to be the case with the amendment to the *Public Education Act* discussed in chapter 1.4 and frequently elsewhere in recent legislation.

As these two analytical perspectives are followed throughout the volume, the concluding remarks will disucss the question of the legitimacy of religion in public life as expressed through recent legislation, more generally, and will relate this to the enabling and disabling mechanisms in such legislation, when considering Islamic communities in context, more specifically.

While this volume of the *Annotated Legal Documents on Islam in Europe* is mostly focused on recent parliamentary legislation, other legal sources are considered too. These include executive orders, official regulations and court rulings of various kinds. Most of the legal texts presented here are directly and explicitly relevant for Islam and Muslims in Denmark, but some are included because of their indirect yet important significance. Such might concern the affairs of the Church of Denmark or certain aspects of illegal coercion and hate crimes. Much of the legislative context reveals that while most provisions are phrased in general terms, they address specific understandings and misunderstandings concerning Islam and Muslims.

Many of the relevant Danish legal texts speak in general language relevant to religion but fail to do so in a neutral way. For this reason the common Danish word for 'priest' or 'preacher' is used in the legal texts but is understood to be generic for priests, ministers, rabbis, imams, hodjas, sheikhs and other religious leaders and spiritual authorities.

The help and support of friends and colleagues must be acknowledged. The continuous encouragement and detailed critique of the full manuscript by Lisbet Christoffersen at the University of Roskilde has as ever been invaluable. The result is so much better for it and I am very grateful. I owe many thanks to

Mikele Schultz-Knudsen, PhD student at the Faculty of Law at the University of Copenhagen, for reading the manuscript and for his comments and suggestions. I owe a debt of gratitude to former Parliamentary Ombudsman Prof. Em. Hans Gammeltoft-Hansen for his feedback. I am grateful to the administration of the Diocese of Copenhagen, in particular Helle Ostenfeld and Marianne Carstensen, for discussing the research in its early phase and for giving me access to their library. Finally, a special word of thanks goes to the editors of the series and at Brill Publishers; as always, I highly appreciate your patience and enjoy working with you.

Any and all errors and misunderstandings in these pages are mine, of course, and will probably continue to bother me long after you have forgotten all about them and this volume.

Niels Valdemar Vinding
May 2020

CHAPTER 1

Status of Religious Communities

From a legal point of view, the Danish Constitutional Act of 1953 (*Danmarks Riges Grundlov*) governs the framework for regulating religious communities in Denmark. Specifically, it governs the relationship between the state, the Church of Denmark and 'the religious communities other than the Evangelical-Lutheran Church of Denmark,' as they are designated in Article 69 of the Constitutional Act (*My Constitutional Act*, 2012, 39). This is done in seven articles of the Constitution, as highlighted below.

Of these, Articles 66 and 69 contain so-called constitutional promises that a constitution will be enacted for the Church and that a statutory framework will be given to regulate other religious communities, generally. In fact, these have remained unchanged since Denmark's first democratic Constitution of 1849. While the constitutional promise to establish the church has yet to be fulfilled, the *Act on Religious Communities outside the Church of Denmark* came into effect on 1 January 2018.

1.1 Constitutional Framework and Guarantees

Since the Constitution of 1849, Denmark has been a democracy. With revisions of state governance structures, the latest in 1953, Denmark has become a secular, liberal democracy with a representative parliament and a monarch as formal head of state, who officially delegates administrative power to a government of political offices, and with an independent judiciary. Notwithstanding the democratic and secular rule of law in Denmark, religion in general and the Church of Denmark specifically feature prominently in the Constitution of the Realm of Denmark dating from 5 June 1953, as amended from the original of 1849.

Danmarks Riges Grundlov af 5. juni 1953.[1]

[…]
§ 4
Den evangelisk-lutherske kirke er den danske folkekirke og understøttes som sådan af staten.

[…]
§ 6
Kongen skal høre til den evangelisk-lutherske kirke.

[…]
§ 66
Folkekirkens forfatning ordnes ved lov.

§ 67
Borgerne har ret til at forene sig i samfund for at dyrke Gud på den måde, der stemmer med deres overbevisning, dog at intet læres eller foretages, som strider mod sædeligheden eller den offentlige orden.

§ 68
Ingen er pligtig at yde personlige bidrag til nogen anden gudsdyrkelse en den, som er hans egen.

§ 69
De fra folkekirken afvigende trossamfunds forhold ordnes nærmere ved lov.

§ 70
Ingen kan på grund af sin trosbekendelse eller afstamning berøves adgang til den fulde nydelse af borgerlige og politiske rettigheder eller unddrage sig opfyldelsen af nogen almindelig borgerpligt.

While the Danish Constitution has been amended several times, most recently in 1953, the "Constitutional law governing relations between State, Church and Religions has not been changed in the 160 years since 1849" (Christoffersen 2010, 147). Freedom of religion and belief is guaranteed in Article 67 and in

1 Danish Constitutional Act, https://www.grundloven.dk/, accessed 1 November 2019.

Denmark there is no legal requirement to register or to seek approval in matters of faith and religion. However, formally there is also no equality of religion, and the Church of Denmark maintains a special position in the Constitution, as per Article 4. In the semi-official English translation of the Constitution published by the Parliament, Article 4 of the Constitution defines the relationship between State and Church as follows: "The Evangelical Lutheran Church shall be the Established Church of Denmark, and as such shall be supported by the State" (*My Constitutional Act* 2012, 3). The Article proclaims the confessional nature of the established church and defines the relationship with the State as being that the latter is committed to supporting the Church financially as well as in other ways. This is explained in the preparatory works for the Constitution. However, a more literal translation is that 'the Evangelical-Lutheran Church is the Danish People's Church and is supported as such by the state.' Note that the church is not called the Church of Denmark, but rather a possession of the 'People'—*People's Church*—so literally, the Danish People's Church. Importantly, the original Danish text does not have the word 'established,' nor does 'Church of Denmark' appear twice, as in the English rendition, but it rather names the Evangelical-Lutheran Church as the People's Church. The language of the Article is performative, and grammatically it is a basic subject complement with the People's Church as the predicative nominal expression that identifies, describes and renames its subject, here the Evangelical-Lutheran Church. As such, legally speaking the Constitutional Act is an Act that transforms the institution from a state church into a People's Church, whose Article 66 then gives the associated promise of legal establishment.

The drafting and preparatory works for the Constitution from the years before 1849 shed some light on what Article 4 means and implies. The key idea of a People's Church, emphasising the literal name for the Evangelical-Lutheran Church of Denmark, presumes that the majority of the people are members of the Church and confess the Evangelical-Lutheran faith. This was of course the case in 1849 with almost 100 per cent membership, but in 2019 the membership is less than 75 per cent (Vinding 2019b). There are several reasons for this, in particular a rising number of individuals of no religion, but other religious groups also make up the difference. In this are included the approximately 320,000 Muslims in Denmark, who constitute just over 5 per cent of the population (Jacobsen and Vinding 2019, 209). Scholars and legal experts have speculated that if—or when—a majority of the population no longer belongs to the Church it would cease to exist as the Danish People's Church. Taking this interpretation to its logical conclusion, it would mean that the state was no longer obliged to support it, financially or otherwise, effectively ending any prospect of proper establishment (Gammeltoft-Hansen 2006, 137).

Of relevance to Muslims as well as other religious communities, commentators note that the obligation to support the Evangelical-Lutheran Church of Denmark does not mean that the state cannot or should not support other religious communities (Gammeltoft-Hansen 2006, 137). This has been a hot topic in Danish public debates, following the argument that Denmark has freedom of religion rather than equality of religions. Lisbet Christoffersen notes that as Denmark guarantees freedom of religion, there is no case for saying that the inequality of the religious communities in Denmark constitutes illegal discrimination. "The system of an established church combined with freedom of religion, yet inequality between religious communities, was accepted as the Danish structure when Denmark ratified the European Convention of Human Rights in 1950" (Christoffersen 2010, 154). However, as we shall see in the following chapters, amongst the legal texts on Islam there are a number of examples of state support and concern for other religious communities in *practical analogy* to that for the rights and privileges of the Evangelical-Lutheran Church of Denmark.

Part seven of the Constitution sets a regulatory frame for religious matters in Articles 66 to 70. Article 66 specifies that "the Constitution of the Evangelical-Lutheran Church of Denmark is regulated by law" (*My Constitutional Act*, 2012, 38). This, in short, is the constitutional promise of establishment that dates back to 1849. Most relevantly, it speaks of a 'constitution' for the Church, rather than just a statutory Act relating to it. Despite five serious attempts by Church commissions and Church councils (1853–1868, 1883–1901, 1928–1939, 1964–1972, and most recently 2012–2014), legal establishment has never come about beyond the administrative practices of the government ministries as part of Danish public and administrative law.[2]

Article 67 of the Constitution states that "[m]embers of the public are entitled to associate in communities to worship God according to their convictions, but nothing may be taught or done that contravenes decency or public order" (*My Consitutional Act*, 2012, 38). This is the positively articulated freedom to associate and to worship, whereas Article 70 negatively defines the guarantee whereby "nobody may be deprived of access to the full enjoyment of civil

2 For a brief discussion of the legislative and constitutional efforts to implement the promise in Article 66 see Vinding, N.V., & Christoffersen, L., *Danish regulation of religion, state of affairs and qualitative reflections* (Centre for European Islamic Thought, Faculty of Theology, University of Copenhagen, 2012), pp. 9–10.

For the most recent of these see Betænkning 1544. Folkekirkens styre. Betænkning fra Udvalget om en mere sammenhængende og moderne styringsstruktur for folkekirken. Ministry of Ecclesiastical Affairs, April 2014.

and political rights or evade the fulfilment of any general civic duty on the grounds of his or her profession of faith" (*My Constitutional Act*, 2012, 39). It is very important from the perspective of Islam and other religious communities in Denmark that there is no obligation to be a member of a specific religious community, let alone the Church of Denmark. In the past, this was an issue for Catholics and Baptists, both before and even in the early years after the Constitution of 1849, where there were some cases of forced baptism and intolerance of religious dissidence. It also follows—and this is articulated in Denmark's ratification of the European Convention on Human Rights—that nobody is to be discriminated against because of their faith or religion, and people may serve in public office irrespective of religious affiliation. In that sense, religion in Denmark is a part of the civil public sphere and people are allowed to gather publicly in worship (Christoffersen 2012, 243). The only justifiable limitation on this freedom is set out in the second part of Article 67, namely, that 'nothing may be taught or done that contravenes decency or public order.' In Denmark, contravening decency or public order is usually taken to mean 'in violation of the law.' However, as former UN Special Rapporteur on freedom of religion and belief, Dr Heiner Bielefeldt, observed in his 2016 report on Denmark, there is increasing political will to pass legislation directing the courts to read this limitation clause more literally, and thereby threaten "to strip Muslim communities from their achieved status position in Denmark or to develop new tools for controlling religions, particularly Islam" (Bielefeldt 2016, 10).

Article 68 declares that "[n]o one shall be liable to make personal contributions to any denomination other than the one to which he adheres." This is a relatively uncontroversial freedom in the Danish Constitution, but there are nonetheless some tensions. For one thing, some see the state support of the Church of Denmark through general taxation as an 'indirect' personal contribution. Such an argument, however, seems rather weak when one considers the Constitution's Article 4. More interestingly, however, for observers interested in Islam and Muslims, there are a number of relatively small, but vocal, organisations in Denmark who claim that buying halal-certified food is such a contribution to denominations other than one's own (cf. Bergeaud-Blackler, Fischer & Lever 2015). The organisations advancing such arguments are not responsive to counter-arguments that buying food on the free market is not a contribution, but rather a deliberate marketing strategy by producers, nor that they are not forced in any way to buy halal products. Nevertheless, it is seen as support for Muslim communities and, much worse, as indirect support for terrorism. From a legal or judicial point of view, the questions of slaughtering and animal ethics have taken priority (Jacobsen 2015, 177) over the question of indirect support.

Specifically in relation to Islam and other minority religions, Article 69 of the Constitution delegated to Parliament the power to pass an Act regulating other religious communities: "[t]he affairs of religious communities other than the Evangelical-Lutheran Church of Denmark are regulated by law." Again, the English translation is more benign than the actual Danish wording, which uses 'deviant' rather than 'other' in understanding the relationship to the state, in obvious contrast to the relationship enjoyed by the Church of Denmark. Here, the affairs of religious communities are the objects of regulation by law, not the communities themselves. Before 2018, no such act had been passed and the promise of regulation by law was seen as analogous to the promise in Article 66. However, a number of rules and regulations did exist to authorise religious clergy and communities to perform weddings with civil legal validity. These rules and regulations amounted to a ministerial executive practice regarding religious communities within the Ministery of Ecclesiastical Affairs and other ministries, which is now in part established in the new *Act on Religious Communities outside the Church of Denmark*.

1.2 Legal Recognition of Churches and Religious Communities

The question of legal recognition of religious communities has recently come to the fore in Denmark. In December 2017, a bill was passed in the Danish Parliament that collected and clarified the rights and privileges applying to the affairs of religious communities outside the Evangelical-Lutheran Church of Denmark. In many ways, this bill ratified many of the existing executive practices in Denmark and gave clear and explicit language to the expectations and privileges of religious communities. Taking effect on 1 January 2018, this new *Act on Religious Communities outside the Church of Denmark* sets the framework for state-religion relations in Denmark, and it does so by legally confirming the executive instruments that confer recognition upon dissenting religious communities as part of statutory law.

Since 1970, rules and regulations to authorise religious clergy and communities to perform ceremonies and weddings were left to the executive practice of the Ministry of Ecclesiastical Affairs and other ministries to govern executively ad hoc and as part of public law, not specifically ecclesiastical law. Religious communities and congregations were divided into three groups: recognised communities, communities with approval to perform weddings with civil legal validity, and other religious communities without any formal recognition. The concept of recognised religious communities originates in pre-constitutional law, as Parliament had not until December 2017 passed any law to enact the promise of Article 69. Until the Marriage Act of 1970, recognition was given by royal decree to communities whose priests were then authorised to perform weddings with civil legal validity and to keep registries of individual status. Such recognition was given to a total of 11 churches and communities, that is, to three Reformed Churches, the Baptist Church, the Methodist Church, the Swedish Gustaf's Church, the Norwegian King Haakon Church, St. Alban's English Church, the Russian Orthodox Church and the Catholic Church, as well as Mosaic Faith Community.

As of 1 January 2018, this three-tier system of recognition, approval and no formal status was significantly changed, as the *Act on Religious Communities outside the Church of Denmark* came into force. The 2018 statute introduces significant new ideas: a legal definition of recognition by ministerial ordinance and distinct mechanisms for revoking the recognition of religious communities. However, as will be discussed below, there are additional noteworthy issues relevant to Islam and Muslims in Denmark.

Lov om trossamfund uden for folkekirken (LOV nr 1533 af 19/12/2017)[3]

Kapitel 1
Definition af trossamfund
§ 1. Ved trossamfund forstås i denne lov et fællesskab, hvis medlemmer samles om en tro på magter, som står over mennesker og naturlove, efter udformede læresætninger og ritualer.

Kapitel 2
Trossamfunds grundlæggende frihed og rettigheder
§ 2. Trossamfund kan frit dannes med ethvert lovligt formål.
§ 3. Et trossamfund har ret til at udøve sin religion, herunder ved overholdelse af religiøse ritualer og skikke samt religiøs undervisning, såfremt der ikke herved opfordres til eller foretages noget, der strider mod bestemmelser fastsat ved lov eller i medfør af lov.
§ 4. Et trossamfund har ret til at udpege personer til at varetage et forkynderembede, rituel ledelse eller tilsvarende.
§ 5. Et trossamfund har ret til at opføre religiøse bygninger. Dette forudsætter, at betingelserne i den øvrige lovgivning om bygningsmæssige krav m.v. er opfyldt.

3 Lov om trossamfund uden for folkekirken, no. 1533, 19/12/2017, https://www.retsinformation.dk/Forms/r0710.aspx?id=196402, accessed 6 January 2019.

§ 6. Et trossamfund kan efter ansøgning til kirkeministeren få tilladelse til at anlægge og drive egne begravelsespladser.
[...]

Kapitel 3
Anerkendelse
§ 7. Et trossamfund kan registreres som anerkendt trossamfund, såfremt det
1) har mindst 50 myndige medlemmer, der enten har fast bopæl i Danmark eller dansk indfødsret, og
2) ikke opfordrer til eller foretager noget, der strider mod bestemmelser i lov eller bestemmelser fastsat i medfør af lov.
Stk. 2. Anmodning om anerkendelse skal indeholde følgende oplysninger:
1) Navn og hjemsted for trossamfundet.
2) Antal myndige medlemmer af trossamfundet.
3) Trossamfundets vedtægter.
4) Navn og adresse på den kontaktperson, der er ansvarlig i forhold til Trossamfundsregistret.
5) En tekst, som udtrykker, beskriver eller henviser til trosgrundlaget eller læretraditionen i trossamfundets religion.
6) Dokumentation for eller beskrivelse af trossamfundets centrale ritualer.
7) Det seneste årsregnskab, som skal være revideret og give et retvisende billede af trossamfundets økonomiske forhold.
[...]

Kapitel 4
Det Rådgivende Udvalg vedrørende Trossamfund
§ 12. Kirkeministeren nedsætter et rådgivende udvalg vedrørende trossamfund. Udvalget består af 4 medlemmer, der besidder sagkundskab inden for henholdsvis religionshistorie, religionssociologi, teologi og retsvidenskab.
[...]

Kapitel 5
Vielsesbemyndigelse m.v.
§ 15. Kirkeministeren kan efter ansøgning fra et anerkendt trossamfund bemyndige en myndig person i trossamfundet til at forrette vielser, jf. § 17, stk. 2, i lov om ægteskabs indgåelse og opløsning.

Stk. 2. Vielsesbemyndigelse, jf. stk. 1, kan enten gives til at foretage en enkelt vielse eller som en stående bemyndigelse til at foretage vielser.
Stk. 3. I forbindelse med ansøgningen skal trossamfundet meddele de relevante oplysninger om den person, der ønskes bemyndiget, jf. § 16.
Stk. 4. Ved ansøgning efter stk. 1 vedlægges trossamfundets vielsesritual. Af ritualet skal det fremgå, at de to personer, der indgår ægteskab, ved samtidigt møde på spørgsmål fra vielsesforretteren skal erklære at ville ægte hinanden og derpå af vielsesforretteren forkyndes at være ægtefolk. Det skal endvidere fremgå eller bekræftes, at vielsen sker i overværelse af mindst to vidner.
Stk. 5. Vielsesritualet må ikke indeholde særlige betingelser for ægteskabet, som strider mod dansk rets regler om myndige personers selvbestemmelsesret, eller som indeholder forskelsbehandling på grund af køn.
Stk. 6. Nærmere regler om fremgangsmåden ved vielse i de anerkendte trossamfund fastsættes af kirkeministeren.
[…]

§ 17. Tildeling af vielsesbemyndigelse skal betinges af, at vielsesforretteren inden 6 måneder efter tildelingen af bemyndigelsen gennemfører et kursus i dansk familieret, frihed og folkestyre.
[…]

Kapitel 6
Tilsyn og tilbagekaldelse af anerkendelse
[…]
§ 22. Opfylder et anerkendt trossamfund ikke længere betingelserne for anerkendelse, eller overholder trossamfundet ikke de forpligtelser, der er fastsat i denne lov, kan kirkeministeren tilbagekalde anerkendelsen.

As something that was previously part of administrative practice, section 1 now legally defines what it means to be a religious community in Denmark. Such a community is now 'a community whose members gather around a belief in powers that are above human beings and the laws of nature, according to designated doctrines and rituals.' This is in accordance with the existing constitutional interpretations and practice of the Advisory Committee on Religious Denominations and with the White Paper of the drafting committee on Religious Communities outside the Church of Denmark, entitled *A coherent legal regulation of Religious Communities outside the Church of Denmark*.[4] In the

4 Betænkning 1564: En samlet lovregulering om andre trossamfund end folkekirken. Kirkem-

White Paper, the drafting committee reveals the three elements constituent to the definition (pp. 75–76). First, the entity needs to be a community and not just individuals' ideas and thoughts. Secondly, the issue of belief or conviction echoes the language of Article 67 of the Constitution and uses a wide understanding of the objects of faith as transcendent powers. However, the definition excludes life-stance communities and associations promoting a certain philosophy of life, as opposed, for example, to the Norwegian understanding of religion and life stance.[5] Thirdly, the drafting committee highlights that such community must act in accordance with designated doctrines and rituals. A fuller legal annotation on this is available in Gammeltoft-Hansen's and Esdahl's commentary on the Act (Gammeltoft-Hansen & Esdahl 2019; Christoffersen 2019b).

Despite the legal establishment in the Act of a definition of religion, this does not resolve some of the continuing issues and problems encountered with applications for recognition from communities that may be borderline. In 2004, the Advisory Committee on Religious Denominations had turned down an application from a football fan club, Copenhagen Lads, by arguing that "not all that resembles religion is religion" (*Afgørelse om 'Copenhagen Lads'*, 2005, 2). Such discussions will continue as the Advisory Committee on Religious Denominations is now also established by section 12 of the Act.[6]

As a move to consolidate, the Act lists the elementary freedoms and rights of religious communities in sections 2 to 6. These include the freedom to pursue lawful purposes, the free exercise and practice of religion by way of such as rituals, customs and teaching within the limits of Article 67 of the Constitution, as well as freedom to appoint religious preachers, erect buildings and run cemeteries. At first glance, such a list seems benign and is understood to be an affirmation of legal rights and freedoms already established. However, it is unclear why there is a need for such a list and what the implicit purpose is. In Danish legislative practice, such examinations and statements of freedoms and

inisteriet, marts 2017. http://www.km.dk/fileadmin/share/nyheder/En_samlet_lovregulering_om_andre_trossamfund_end_folkekirken.pdf, accessed 1 November 2019.

5 Cf. Bøe, Marianne, *Annotated Legal Documents on Islam in Norway* (Leiden: Brill, 2018), pp. 7–11.

6 For a fuller discussion of the work and issues of the Advisory Committee on Religious Denominations see Vinding, Niels Valdemar, *Muslim Positions in the Religio-organisational fields of Denmark, Germany and England*, (Copenhagen: Faculty of Theology, 2013), chapter 5 "The Advisory Committee on Religious Denominations, Danish Muslim Organisations and the fundamental dividers in the religio-organisational field in Denmark."

rights are included in the drafting comments attached to the bill, but this statement is explicit in the Act itself. Lisbet Christoffersen argues that the purpose is not to be declarative but rather to use the definition to admonish religious communities, because to make clear such freedoms and rights is also to restate their limits.[7] Such a view is highly relevant for the discussion of much of the other legislation in the light of which section 2 of this Act may be seen as an exhortation to Muslims or religious minorities to follow the law—perhaps as they would otherwise implicitly be assumed not to.

In this light, the Act continues to regulate the rules of recognition in section 7, and later the ministerial oversight of religious communities and the rules for rescinding the recognition. As may be argued, the recognition established here marks a significant improvement for Muslims and Islamic communities in Denmark, as they are now recognised and not merely approved.[8] This places Islamic communities as well as other previously approved religious communities on an equal footing with the oldest recognised religious communities, such as the Catholic and Jewish communities.

As part of the preliminary work for the drafting of the statute, the Committee on Religious Communities outside the Church of Denmark was set up to prepare the mentioned White Paper on the legislative potential for fulfilling the constitutional promise made in Article 69. Between February 2015 and February 2017, this Committee on Religious Communities held 15 meetings and invited several of the recognised and approved congregations and religious communities to discuss its work. In its White Paper, the Committee discusses in detail the idea and meaning of 'recognition' in the Danish context, as it ties the legal position of religious communities closely to the right to perform valid civil marriages. On legal recognition of religious communities, the Committee writes:

> Recognition as a religious community gives the religious community special economic privileges and the chance to be delegated a public jurisdictional authority with regard to the right to perform valid civil marriages. This Committee understands that, in return for these special rights, the state may require the religious community to function in a way that meets—or at least is not in direct conflict with—fundamental societal

---

7 https://baptist.dk/trossamfundsloven-og-religionsfrihed/ accessed 1 November 2019.

8 Vinding, "Godkendelse og anerkendelse af de islamiske trossamfund i Danmark", in *Trossamfundslov. Blasfemibestemmelse. Kirkeretsantologi 2019*, Christoffersen, L., Andersen, S., & Jørgensen, A. (eds) (Copenhagen: Forlaget Eksistensen for Selskab for Kirkeret, 2019).

values, including democratic ideals, as well as the fundamental principles of law applicable to the exercise of public authority.[9]

In this regard, one particular detail in the new law might raise some concerns with Muslim communities. A problematising reading of section 15, subsection 5, of the *Act on Religious Communities outside the Church of Denmark* might see it as indirectly addressing Muslim practice—or rather—misgivings about assumed Muslim practices. "The marriage ritual must not contain any special conditions for marriage, which contravene Danish law's rules on the right of self-determination of persons, or which involve discrimination on grounds of gender." The commentary to the Act specifically mentions that the Act deals with the situation where "the female party must have the consent of male witnesses," echoing the institution of guardian (*wali*) in Islam, which is interpreted and put into practice in many different ways and not necessarily a 'condition' or a limit to 'self-determination.' If read literally, even fathers who walked their daughters down the aisle of the church and presented them to their husbands-to-be could be seen as giving a kind of determining approval and would be within the scope of the section. However, in their commentary to the law, Gammeltoft-Hansen and Esdahl argue that the section is aimed at cases of, for instance, the marriage of minors or forced marriages, or cases where the female party must have the explicit consent of male witnesses or guardians (Gammeltoft-Hansen & Esdahl 2019, 69).

1.3 Registered Religious Communities

Under the *Act on the processing of personal data* (LOV nr 429 af 31/05/2000), which has now been superseded by the Danish implementation of the European Union's General Data Protection Regulation (EU, 2016/679), it was illegal to collect data on race or ethnicity, political, religious or philosophical beliefs, union affiliation, health and sexual relations. The current iteration of this prohibition is contained in the Act on Data Protection (LOV nr 502 af 23/05/2018), which states:

Lov om supplerende bestemmelser til forordning om beskyttelse af fysiske personer i forbindelse med behandling af personoplysninger og om fri

9 *Betænkning 1564: En samlet lovregulering om andre trossamfund end folkekirken*, Copenhagen 2017, p. 38, author's translation.

udveksling af sådanne oplysninger (databeskyttelsesloven) (LOV nr 502 af 23/05/2018)[10]
[…]

Artikel 9
Behandling af særlige kategorier af personoplysninger
1. Behandling af personoplysninger om race eller etnisk oprindelse, politisk, religiøs eller filosofisk overbevisning eller fagforeningsmæssigt tilhørsforhold samt behandling af genetiske data, biometriske data med det formål entydigt at identificere en fysisk person, helbredsoplysninger eller oplysninger om en fysisk persons seksuelle forhold eller seksuelle orientering er forbudt.

The 'processing of personal information on race or ethnic origins, political, religious or philosophical convictions … is [expressly] forbidden.' This means that unless under an express agreement and duly anonymised, or for reasons of state security or criminal prosecution and so forth, no public authority, business or private body may collect, process or register such information. In Denmark, this means that there can be no public census asking individuals to specify their political or religious affiliation, and that there can be no public registration of members of religious communities. Organisations and communities that undertake legitimate religious activities may of course register their members and, if approved, the community should maintain a list of members which the ministry may be allowed to consult. Thus, for the religious communities who of their own volition seek the recognition of the state as discussed above there is now a Registry of Religious Communities in Denmark. This keeps a register of communities, not of persons associated with them, although membership lists should be available on demand. Until the *Act on Religious Communities outside the Church of Denmark* was enacted, there had been only a very loose framework for any control or inspection of the communities. Before the Act, it had been only in theory that the ministry had the power to rescind or withdraw recognition, and so no systematic register of religious communities was maintained.

In section 7, subsection 4, the Act sets up the Registry of Religious Communities: "[r]ecognition is entered in the Registry of Religions Communities, which is comes under the Ministry of Ecclesiastical Affairs." This paragraph lays down a number of continuing duties that the communities must adhere to, including

10 https://www.retsinformation.dk/Forms/r0710.aspx?id=201319, accessed 1 November 2019.

the making of annual reports and submitting their constitutions and articles of association to the ministry.

This power to control or inspect religious communities is regulated by the *Executive Order on the Registry of Religious Communities* from 15 November 2018,

> Bekendtgørelse om Trossamfundsregistret (BEK nr 1283 af 15/11/2018)[11]
> […]
>
> Kapitel 2
> *Trossamfundsregistrets formål, indretning og førelse*
>
> § 3. Trossamfundsregistret har til formål at sikre en lettere adgang til indsigt i, hvilke trossamfund der er anerkendt, og hvilke menigheder der er omfattet af et trossamfunds anerkendelse, samt indsigt i deres økonomiske og organisatoriske forhold.
>
> § 4. Når et trossamfund med evt. tilhørende menigheder er blevet anerkendt, opretter Kirkeministeriet en særskilt 'side' for henholdsvis trossamfund og den enkelte menighed i Trossamfunds-registret, der giver trossamfundet og evt. tilhørende menigheder adgang til at indberette oplysninger om de i §§ 10 og 11 anførte forhold.

As the order clearly states, the purpose of the Registry of Religious Communities is to ensure easier access and information as to which religious communities are recognised and which congregations are part of those religious communities. Also included is a requirement of transparency regarding their financial and organisational affairs. This is done at the website[12] of the Ministry of Ecclesiastical Affairs, where a separate 'page' lists the articles of association, the central rituals and the articles of faith of each religious community and individual congregation. As of 31 October 2019, all 28 recognised Islamic religious communities have uploaded this information and as an obligatory part of this they have filed details of financial information, audited accounts and donations.

11 https://www.retsinformation.dk/Forms/R0710.aspx?id=204953, accessed 1 November 2019.

12 https://www.km.dk/andre-trossamfund/trossamfundsregistret/liste-over-anerkendte-trossamfund-og-tilknyttede-menigheder/, accessed 1 February 2020.

While the establishment and upkeep of the Registry of Religious Communities seems to be straightforward and quite benign, there is no doubt of the potential risks that such a registry might entail. Not only do religious communities, especially smaller communities, see the keeping of a register as a significant disadvantage and burden in their work, but it is also clearly understood as a means of questioning their legitimacy and loyalty to democracy, the rule of law and public order. The Turkish community argues that any local chairman, member of a mosque's board or its imam who violated laws or spoke against democracy would also be in violation of its own articles of association.[13] In addition, there is reason for concern about the general idea of keeping a register of religious communities. Former Special Rapporteur on freedom of religious or belief, Heiner Bielefledt, warns in his 2011 report against such registration.

> All registration decisions must be based on clearly defined formal elements of law and in conformity with international law. Registration should neither depend on extensive formal requirements in terms of numbers of members and the time a particular community has existed, nor should it depend on the review of the substantive content of the belief, structure of the community and methods of appointment of the clergy.[14]

In this regard, it is important to restate that in Denmark there is no requirement for religious communities to register and that such communities enjoy the full freedom of religion and belief without any form of public registration. Heiner Bielefeldt warns against practices which make registration and state approval a condition of religious communities enjoying the status of a legal entity. This is not the case in Denmark. However, a practice of registration of religious communities is in danger of bringing about a differentiation between such communities. Bielefeldt warns against any kind of privileged status among religious communities. His reasoning must be understood as a protection of religious freedom and a move towards anti-discrimination and formal equality. Even the slightest distortion of such principles might lead to discrimination.

---

13 E.g. Danish-Turkish Islamic Foundation, *Høring vedrørende den nye trossamfundslov*. 2017.

14 Bielefeldt 2011, "Report of the Special Rapporteur on freedom of religion or belief," (A/HCR/19/60), 22 December 2011, p. 20. For a discussion on this see Vinding 2012, 300–302.

The ultimate risk of the registration of religious communities is highlighted by the Jewish Community in Denmark.[15] They note their appreciation of the fact that religious communities are not required to send their membership lists to the ministry. To require that would, of course, echo the very horrible history of the holocaust, and the Jewish Community 'nervously' warns against Parliament ever enacting legislation that would lead down a similar path because of 'fleeting populist trends' or animosity against religious practice.

1.4 Religious Communities as Associations

As a key part of the legislative programme that was announced in the 'Agreement Paper' of 31 May 2016, the then Minister of Cultural and Ecclesiastical Affairs, Bertel Haarder, insisted that the agreeing parties would combat any "behaviour that sought to undermine Danish laws and values and support parallel law." Furthermore, they "want to cut off funding for individuals who might demonstrate such behaviour and who have previously been financially or legally supported by state or municipality. We do not want to be ridiculed at our own expense."[16]

This assumption that some communities or individuals seeking 'to undermine Danish laws and values and support parallel law" are also being financially supported by municipalities or state subsidies had lingered in some political circles for quite a while. Nevertheless, it was the controversial TV documentary, 'Mosques behind the Veil,' that sparked the political anger of the Minister of Cultural and Ecclesiastical Affairs and the parties behind the agreement. The documentary had sought to reveal that certain individuals and organisations had illegally or illegitimately obtained financial support and had used it to further their malevolent agendas. While the TV documentary was criticised for the portrait it painted of the communities and its editing, nevertheless legislators took the opportunity offered by the documentary to put forward legislation that would strike hard against financial support for religious organisations and associations at the municipal level.

On 5 October 2016, the Minister of Cultural and Ecclesiastical Affairs, Bertel Haarder, proposed a bill to amend both the *Public Education Act* and the *Tax Assessment Act*. The Bill seeks to take legislative action against associations that oppose or undermine democracy or fundamental freedoms and human rights. It was passed on 6 December 2016.

15 *Det Jødiske Samfund i Danmark*, Høring over udkast til forslag til Lov om trossamfund uden for folkekirken, Copenhagen, 30 August 2017.

16 Agreement paper 31 May 2016, op. cit.

Lov om ændring af folkeoplysningsloven og ligningsloven[17]
(Indsats mod foreninger, som modarbejder eller underminerer demokrati eller grundlæggende friheds- og menneskerettigheder) (LOV nr 1553 af 13/12/2016)
[…]

§ 4 a. Foreninger, hvis formål eller adfærd modarbejder eller underminerer demokrati eller grundlæggende friheds og menneskerettigheder, kan ikke ydes tilskud eller anvises lokaler efter denne lov.
[…]

§ 33, stk. 4, ophæves, og i stedet indsættes:
Stk. 4. Der kan ikke ydes tilskud til aktiviteter, som har karakter af gudsdyrkelse eller kirkelige handlinger.
Stk. 5. Kommunalbestyrelsen fører tilsyn med, at foreninger, der modtager tilskud eller anvises lokaler efter denne lov, overholder loven eller regler fastsat i medfør heraf. Kommunalbestyrelsen kan forlange hel eller delvis tilbagebetaling af udbetalt tilskud, standse udbetaling af tilskud eller tilbageholde udbetaling af tilskud helt eller delvis og fratage foreninger retten til at benytte allerede anviste lokaler, hvis foreningerne ikke overholder loven eller regler fastsat i medfør heraf, jf. dog stk. 7.

In relatively direct language, the amendment provides in section 4 that associations whose purpose or behaviour contravenes or undermines democracy or fundamental freedoms and human rights cannot be given subsidies or assigned premises. In addition, the new section 33, subsection 4, explicitly states that activities for the purpose of worship or religious ceremonies cannot be supported, and subsection 5 delegates to the municipalities the power to ensure that no associations are incorrectly subsidised or supported. While the language of the amendment may be clear, the drafting notes and comments by the ministry demonstrate that enacting the clear political will and enforcing its provisions are highly problematic and test the limits of valid legislation. As a case in point, the drafting notes and comments highlight that the amendment is to live up to the aforementioned agreement paper, by "seeking solutions to the fundamental challenge that there are in Denmark religious preachers who abuse their freedoms to preach hatred and undermine the society in which

17 https://www.ft.dk/samling/20161/lovforslag/l13/som_vedtaget.htm, accessed 1 November 2019.

they should be a part," adding that "this is a complex challenge that is found in other Western countries."[18] However, such a claim and general allusion are entirely political and not in any way substantiated by the ministry beyond being described as a fundamental challenge. The *ratio legis* seems to be based on a political fiction.

Further, the ministry highlights the motivations and considerations of the Government in proposing the Bill. At the time of its proposal, any association that lived up to the specific conditions would qualify for support regardless of whether 'that association, in other contexts, calls for the abolition of democracy or fundamental freedoms and human rights.'[19] In such a situation, the government finds that there is no clear regulation on whether the municipalites may deny such support. Then, the motivation is revealed:

> The Government finds such a legal state of affairs unacceptable. Thus, in the Government's view, it should not be the case that an association on the one hand can agitate to abolish democracy or fundamental freedoms and human rights and, on the other hand, arrange for municipal subsidies under the Public Education Act, for example, to arrange a football academy for young people risking the association's extreme attitudes in this connection being passed on to the young people in question.[20]

This then leaves to the ministry's lawyers to implement such political will and particular view of the world in actual legislation and to guide the municipalities in their enforcement of the changes regarding the inspection of associations. The Bill hinges on three understandings of 'democracy,' 'elemental freedoms and human rights' and what it means to 'counteract or undermine' democracy, and the ministry reveals not just its understanding of such concepts, but also of

18 Ministry of Culture, "Lovforslag nr. L13, Forslag til Lov om ændring af folkeoplysningsloven og ligningsloven, som fremsat," i Folketingstidende A, Folketinget 2016–2017, p. 5, https://www.ft.dk/ripdf/samling/20161/lovforslag/l13/20161_l13_som_fremsat.pdf, accessed 1 July 2019.

19 Ministry of Culture, "Lovforslag nr. L13, Forslag til Lov om ændring af folkeoplysningsloven og ligningsloven, som fremsat," i Folketingstidende A, Folketinget 2016–2017, p. 7, https://www.ft.dk/ripdf/samling/20161/lovforslag/l13/20161_l13_som_fremsat.pdf, accessed 1 July 2019.

20 Ministry of Culture, "Lovforslag nr. L13, Forslag til Lov om ændring af folkeoplysningsloven og ligningsloven, som fremsat," i Folketingstidende A, Folketinget 2016–2017, p. 7, https://www.ft.dk/ripdf/samling/20161/lovforslag/l13/20161_l13_som_fremsat.pdf, accessed 1 July 2019.

what violations and infractions might look like, again, highly speculative and not substantiated by case law or real-world examples.

> *3.1.3.2.1.* The term "democracy" is to be understood as a rule of government with representative democracy, where power is divided into legislative, executive and judicial powers. Activities that, for example, encourage the abolition of the Danish people's government or decisively change this, including by democratic means, will thus be covered by the bill. It can be statements that express support and seek to endorse the introduction of caliphate or dictatorship in this country.[21]

The endorsement concerning the introduction of the caliphate is highlighted expressly. It does not matter whether the association is operating democratically, but with another system of government as an end, such as a left-wing political association that talks of revolution or, as is the case here, a party like Hizb ut-Tahrir. No such organisations, parties or political options are forbidden in Denmark, but after this amendment they cannot gain municipal support. Soon after the Bill was enacted, Copenhagen Municipality denied Hizb ut-Tahrir the use of a gym hall with reference to the 'anti-democratic' attitudes of Hizb ut-Tahrir.[22]

To the jurists in the Ministry of Culture

> [t]he concept of 'fundamental freedoms and human rights' refers to the fundamental freedoms and human rights that flow from the constitution and the European Convention on Human Rights. This is, for example, freedom of expression, freedom of association, freedom of assembly, religious freedom, the right to life, the prohibition of torture, the right to a fair trial and private property. Activities that, for example, encourage the abolition or significant restrictions of fundamental rights such as freedom of expression or religious freedom, will thus be regulated by the proposed provision.[23]

---

21 Ministry of Culture, "Lovforslag nr. L13, Forslag til Lov om ændring af folkeoplysningsloven og ligningsloven, som fremsat," i Folketingstidende A, Folketinget 2016–2017, p. 8, https://www.ft.dk/ripdf/samling/20161/lovforslag/l13/20161_l13_som_fremsat.pdf, accessed 1 July 2019.

22 https://www.tv2lorry.dk/artikel/hizb-ut-tahrir-vil-leje-noerrebrohallen-men-vil-kommune-afvise-med-ny-lov, accessed 1 November 2019.

23 Ministry of Culture, "Lovforslag nr. L13, Forslag til Lov om ændring af folkeoplysningsloven

Finally, the ministry explains what it means by counteracting or undermining, and it does not limit its interpretation to deliberate actions or direct threats. It also includes indirect harm or hindrance to or weakening of the democratic attitudes of vulnerable groups in its care or attending their organised activities.

Such attempts to clarify or define conceptually the operable ideas in the Bill cannot stand alone, and thus the ministry offers a series of examples of actions, attitudes and sentiments that might counteract or undermine democracy and, by way of contrast, of what does not.

It highlights, for example,[24]

> statements that Danish democracy should be abolished and replaced by a caliphate state or calls to break the law or to generally refrain from using its voting rights

and

> calls to use religious courts to make decisions on the basis of religious writings and dogmas instead of and contrary to the laws adopted by the Parliament.

and

> statements that censorship or a general prohibition of religious criticism should be introduced or that women should generally not be allowed to work or otherwise participate in community life on equal terms with men.

However, the ministry does draw a line for what criticisms might be acceptable in a democracy and what may be found to be within the limits of public debate and of educational interest to the public.

---

og ligningsloven, som fremsat," i Folketingstidende A, Folketinget 2016–2017, p. 8, https://www.ft.dk/ripdf/samling/20161/lovforslag/l13/20161_l13_som_fremsat.pdf, accessed 1 July 2019.

24 This quote and below, from Ministry of Culture, "Lovforslag nr. L13, Forslag til Lov om ændring af folkeoplysningsloven og ligningsloven, som fremsat," i Folketingstidende A, Folketinget 2016–2017, pp. 8–9, https://www.ft.dk/ripdf/samling/20161/lovforslag/l13/20161_l13_som_fremsat.pdf, accessed 1 July 2019.

> On the other hand, critical statements about the state of the Danish people's government, including critical statements about the incumbent government, the policy pursued or the relationship between the Folketing and the government will clearly fall outside the scope of the provision. The same applies to criticism of specific decisions by the courts.

and

> It is not every act that seeks to promote a point of view that is contrary to democracy or fundamental freedoms and human rights which will be covered by the bill, the act of which must be intended or intended to counteract or undermine democracy or fundamental freedoms and human rights. Thus, it will not be covered by the bill if an association, for example, argues that expulsion rules should be tightened in a way that would not be compatible with the European Court of Human Rights case law on the right to respect for family life.

and

> The same is true of statements that men or women should not hold certain positions, e.g. as a priest.

All these examples appear to be hypothetical and are not substantiated by the ministry by reference to any documented issues or to the practice of the courts. Taken together, they read like a paraphrase of a biased and limited perception of ideas and expressions associated with Islam or immigrant communities. Considering the political climate in Denmark at the time of the passing of the legislation as well as the very clear governmental motivation for proposing the Bill in the first place, it seems that the perception and understanding of Islam conveyed therein is a poor and biased echo of Islam as articulating anti-freedom in an interpretation of 'submission,' Islamic courts as a subversive legal order, or anti-democratic sentiments embedded in the idea of Allah as the ultimate legislator. Simply put, it seems that the government politicians and drafting jurists are regurgitating Islamist propaganda rather than considering the legal facts of the reality they wish to regulate.

Unsurprisingly, the Bill and the ministerial drafting notes and comments drew criticism from religious communities, legal professional organisations and leading legal minds.

Lisbet Christoffersen points to the obvious incoherencies in targeting the "use of religious courts to decide on the basis of religious writings and dogmas instead of and contrary to the laws," which also questions the very well-established practice of the canonical courts of the Catholic Church in Denmark, the international legal order of the Methodists (Christoffersen 2019a), the Mosaic community and its rabbinical court, and the Orthodox communities. She adds St Alban's Anglican Church in Copenhagen, which explicitly follows the canons of the Church of England (Christoffersen 2016).

Advokatrådet (The Council of the Danish Bar and Law Society) also argued against the Bill. It pointed to the explicit bias and incoherence in the choice of examples of what is allowed and what is not, which will in effect make it impossible for the local municipalities to uphold the law (Advokatrådet 2016a). In addition, it considers that the rules will be "incredibly difficult to manage in practice, which would mean an increased risk of incorrect rulings," and that they were very worried from the point of view of the rule of law. It recommended that a legislative or legal advisory committee be set up to examine this and other bills under the same intiative.

The *Institut for Menneskerettigheder* (Danish Institute for Human Rights) points to the poor legislative quality in the fact that the Bill has not considered the impact on Denmark's commitment to international human rights.[25] This is not just a problem for the government, but also for the municipalities, who may be admonished for not duly considering human rights and international commitments.

Considering these significant concerns in the light of the speculative and biased examples given by the government and the drafting jurists at the ministry, it seems that the law is nearly impossible to administer—due either to the technical problems of interpreting its principles or to the risk of violating humans rights, or simply the risk of unduly supporting Islamist and other forbidden organisations. Ultimately, the consequence might be that the municipalities withhold funding under the Public Education Act to the detriment of public education generally, and to migrant or faith-based associations that might need such funding more than most in their efforts to integrate and offer public education.

---

25 Dansk Institut for Menneskerettigheder, 2016, "Høringssvar til L13."

CHAPTER 2

Relations between the State and Islam

2.1 Introduction

The relationship between the state and Islam is understood most clearly in the light of the Constitution and the recent legislation in the form of the *Act on Religious Communities outside the Church of Denmark*. The Church of Denmark is by far the most significant and important religious community in Denmark, and most of the relations between state and Islam are regulated in the light of the majority church. This is a general condition for most, if not all, religious communities in Denmark. Rights that the Church of Denmark holds, and which are not in their nature specific to that institution, are by analogy extended to other religious communities. Considering the relationship between the state, the Church of Denmark and other religious communities—including Islamic communities—it is clear that there is a hierarchy of levels in the socio-legal structures.

At the top of the hierarchy and with the closest relationship with the state we find the Church of Denmark.[1] This is rooted in the Constitution, and although Parliamentary statutes to regulate the Church were never agreed upon, the state is committed to supporting the Church, its clergy are public servants and the state collects church taxes. Not just by way of the constitutional provisions, but also in a lot of subsequent legislation, Parliament regulates the general, public law for the Church as well as the specific regulations for Church finances, buildings, employment, organisation and so on. In 2016, a preparatory committee drafted a White Paper which addressed 'a more coherent and modern governance structure for the Church of Denmark,' and drafted a suggestion for what a fulfilment of the constitutional promise in Article 66 might look like.[2] This did not result in legislation (Christoffersen 2019b).

Second in the hierarchy of state-religion relations are the bulk of the recognised religious communities, which includes Islamic communities. These are now regulated under the *Act on Religious Communities outside the Church of Denmark*, as discussed above. Recognition is not very clearly defined in its legal nature but implies degrees of mutuality or reciprocity and a number of

1 For a fuller discussion of the three hierarchical levels in the Danish regulation of religion, see Vejrup Nielsen 2012.

2 http://www.km.dk/fileadmin/share/Styringsstruktur/Betaenkning_1544.pdf.

privileges embedded in that relationship. Silvio Ferrari noted in 2002 in a discussion on "Islam and the Western European Model of Church and State Relations"[3] that co-operation between religious communities, on the one hand, and state and government bodies, on the other, is one of the most important contemporary regulatory regimes in Europe. "Generally speaking," Ferrari argues "co-operation is broader where the central principles and values of a religious group are in accordance with the principles and values shared by the majority of the [...] society" (Ferrari 2002, 10). In his 2002 article, Ferrari speaks of this second group and notes that it is defined and "regulated by special laws enacted for religious associations" (Ferrari 2002, 10), and that entering into this category of cooperation requires 'registration or recognition' and 'some kind of State control,' which includes a degree of selectivity on behalf of the state. In Denmark, such selection is of course based on objective criteria and the free submission of applications for recognition. As becomes clear in much of the legislation discussed in this volume and in the previous and present chapters, this observation indeed applies in Denmark.

Some religious communities are not included in the second category and thus relegated to the third category of those communities which either do not live up to the standards of recognition or exercise their freedom not to apply for recognition. This category "includes all religious activity that does not enter into formalised relations to [*sic*] the state and is regulated only by general laws ..." (Vejrup Nielsen 2012, 45).

In Denmark there is no one general law, agreement or 'concordat' that regulates the relations between the state and Islam, but we may find aspects of such relations in different distinct legal documents. Something similar may be said of the principles that may regulate state-Islam relations in Denmark, and we are currently witnessing a deliberative process negotiating the role and requirements of Islam and Muslims in Denmark, some of which are being and will be legally regulated.

In 2012 as part of the RELIGARE international research consortium,[4] Vinding and Christoffersen published a research report on *Danish Regulation of Religion, State of Affairs and Qualitative Reflections*, which set out to investigate this exact question of the legal regulation of religion in Denmark and present the state of affairs to Danish and international colleagues and stakeholders. The structure of the report followed an analytical strategy of sets of basic tensions

---

3 Ferrari 2002 on "Islam and the Western European Model of Church and State Relations," which is discussed at greater length in Vinding 2013, pp. 96–102.

4 Funded under the European Commission's FP7-SSH programme with grant agreement no. 244635, which ended on 30 April 2013.

between religion and secularity in Denmark. The conclusions highlighted that across state and societal sectors Danish regulation of religion was characterised by a great degree of secularisation and reasonable and ad hoc accommodation of minority religious concerns. Problems and tensions are of course part of the everyday life of religious groups in a secular country, but such problems are mostly resolved constructively. While only a few legal institutions and measures are put into effect to monitor violations of religious rights in Denmark, such as the Board of Equal Treatment and the Danish Institute for Human Rights, the report concludes that 'legal norms and instruments do not seem to be the most appropriate tools to solve these conflicts' (Vinding & Christoffersen 2012, 142). Rather, a significant degree of debate and deliberation on the issue of religion in the public space, including Islam and Muslims, is taking place. This may at times border on the polemical and racist or islamophobic but, generally speaking, a national conversation is unfolding about the proper place, participation and regulation of Islam in Denmark. Such a discourse is deliberative in nature. Danish historical roots are deep and the close relations between state, church and society are embedded mono-culturally, mono-ethnically and mono-religiously. As the report notes, the relationship of religion and society "has to be reformed softly, slowly, and through public deliberation in order to maintain the values worth protecting and to change what needs to be changed" (Vinding & Christoffersen 2012, 142).

2.2 General Provisions Relevant to Religion

As highlighted above, a number of very specific legal acts and executive orders regulate or have general implications for religious communities, including Islamic communities. One such example is from the law regarding membership of the Church of Denmark, ecclesiastical services and the freedom to move parish, most recently revised in 2012.

Bekendtgørelse af lov om medlemskab af folkekirken, kirkelig betjening og sognebåndsløsning (LBK nr 622 af 19/06/2012)[5]

Kapitel 1
Stiftelse og ophør af medlemskab af folkekirken

5 https://www.retsinformation.dk/Forms/R0710.aspx?id=142350, accessed 1 November 2019.

§ 1. Personer, der døbes i folkekirken, bliver ved dåben medlem af folkekirken.
Stk. 2. Personer, der er døbt i et andet evangelisk-luthersk trossamfund her i landet, bliver medlem af folkekirken ved at slutte sig til en menighed i folkekirken.
Stk. 3. Personer, der er døbt i et evangelisk-luthersk trossamfund i udlandet, bliver medlem af folkekirken ved at tage ophold her i landet, medmindre de anmelder at ville stå uden for folkekirken.
Stk. 4. Andre personer, der er døbt med den kristne dåb, bliver medlem af folkekirken ved at optages i folkekirken eller for mindreåriges vedkommende ved at opdrages i folkekirkens tro.
§ 2. Et medlem af folkekirken kan bringe sit medlemskab til ophør ved skriftlig anmeldelse.
Stk. 2. Medlemskabet ophører, såfremt et medlem slutter sig til et andet trossamfund eller på anden måde, f.eks. ved at lade sig gendøbe, stiller sig uden for folkekirken.
[…]

§ 4. Ministeren for ligestilling og kirke fastsætter nærmere regler om optagelse i og udtræden af folkekirken.

Here, it is clearly established that only people who are baptised either as specifically Evangelical-Lutheran or generally Christian may become members of the Church of Denmark. If foreigners are baptised Evangelical-Lutheran, they automatically join the Church and have Church taxes collected from them, unless they opt out, which must be done in writing, or if they actively join another religious community. The Minister of Ecclesiastical Affairs retains the prerogative to specify the rules regarding membership of the Church of Denmark.

For immigrants, foreigners, refugees or legal aliens in general, or Muslims specifically, this might seem relevant only if they are or want to be Evangelical-Lutheran. However, a number of cases have been reported of people being automatically added as members of the Church and ending up involuntarily paying Church taxes when they take up residency. That is, until they discover the fact on their tax returns. According to observers and press stories from 2009, this was illegal and considered a systemic error.[6] However, it speaks to the issues

6 *Berlingske Tidene*, 4 May 2009, "Udlændinge betaler ufrivillig kirkeskat," https://www.berlingske.dk/samfund/udlaendinge-betaler-ufrivillig-kirkeskat, accessed 1 November 2019.

that might arise in a legal system that is managed in close relation to the Church of Denmark, where membership is considered an automatic default position. However, it is important to note that the error is perpetrated not by the administration of the church, but by the municipal services.

Another three examples of general legal implications for Islam and Muslims in Denmark are found in the *Procedural Code*, as amended in 2017.

Bekendtgørelse af lov om rettens pleje (LBK nr 1101 af 22/09/2017)[7]
(*Retsplejeloven*)

§ 56. En dommer må i retsmøder ikke fremtræde på en måde, der er egnet til at blive opfattet som en tilkendegivelse om den pågældendes eventuelle religiøse eller politiske tilhørsforhold eller om den pågældendes holdning til religiøse eller politiske spørgsmål i øvrigt.
Stk. 2. Stk. 1 finder tilsvarende anvendelse på fuldmægtige, midlertidigt beskikkede dommere og de personer, der er nævnt i § 19, stk. 3.
[…]

§ 70. Følgende personer er udelukket fra at være nævning og domsmand:
1) Ministre,
2) ansatte i ministeriers departementer og ansatte i chefstillinger i de under departementerne hørende underordnede myndigheder,
3) ansatte ved domstolene og i politiet, anklagemyndigheden, kriminalforsorgen og andre myndigheder på Justitsministeriets område,
4) advokater og advokatfuldmægtige og
5) præster i folkekirken og andre trossamfund.
[…]

Kapitel 18
Vidner
§ 170. Mod dens ønske, som har krav på hemmeligholdelse, må vidneforklaring ikke afkræves præster i folkekirken eller andre trossamfund, læger, forsvarere, retsmæglere og advokater om det, som er kommet til deres kundskab ved udøvelsen af deres virksomhed.

The *Procedural Code* regulates the judiciary and here the examples are relevant to Islam and Muslims.

7 https://www.retsinformation.dk/Forms/R0710.aspx?id=209542, accessed 1 November 2019.

Firstly, in Article 56 it demands that judges appear neutral. This is a highly controversial Article as it threatens to overregulate the decorum and independence of the judiciary. This is discussed further in chapter 14 on *Islamic dress*.

Secondly, in Article 70 the Code bans religious personnel, i.e. 'priests in the Church of Denmark and other religious communities,' from sitting on juries or working as lay judges. This was added as an amendment in 2017 after a significant outcry amongst conservative and right-wing populist politicians as they realised that religious communities, which were not recognised were not regulated by Article 70. In their legislative imagination, they considered cases where an imam might sit on a jury or even function as a lay judge and possibly rule according to their Sharia law.[8] This found resonance in the left-wing argument that no religious personnel should be eligible to serve, and thus the change came into effect in 2017. However, it is worth noting that the *ratio legis* for not having priests is entirely other than such suspicions of a parallel legal order might assume. The rule is based in the fact that in the legal order from before the Constitution priests had significant sensitive knowledge, considerable administrative powers and confessional privilege, all of which are incompatible with being jury members or lay judges. This is the same rationale as that behind prohibiting others, such as government ministers, prosecutors, and lawyers, from serving.

Thirdly, Article 170 specifies that 'priests in the Church of Denmark and other religious communities' have an extended degree of confidentiality and cannot be made to testify against their will, except in national security and similar issues. This is similar to the confidentiality that doctors and attourneys enjoy. This provision originates in the *Danish Code* of 1683 and establishes the confessional or confidential conversation with a priest of the Church as inviolable. Here the banal analogy between priests in the Church of Denmark and other religious communities works to the remarkable benefit of religious personel in other religious communities, as will be further discussed in chapter 10 on *Islamic chaplaincy in public institutions*.

8 "L149, Forslag til lov om ændring af retsplejeloven," https://www.ft.dk/samling/20161/lovforslag/l149/beh1-70/forhandling.htm, accessed 1 November 2019.

CHAPTER 3

State Support for Islamic Religious Communities

As is clear from Article 4 of the Constitution, the Danish state supports the Church of Denmark, both directly through funding and indirectly through tax collection, organisational support, employment and the like. Chapter 6 in Vinding & Christoffersen's 2012 report investigated this state support for religion in Denmark.[1] The report highlights that much of the complexity in this area concerns the Church of Denmark, because the regulation of legal competences to decide on ownership, rights and the rationales behind the status quo is unresolved.

Regarding other religious communities generally, and Islamic communities in particular, the legal state of affairs is a little simpler, although the courts have needed to decide on questions of equality, the constitutionality of state support and freedom of religion.[2] Again, here it is worth noting that while this is highly and specifically relevant to Islamic communities and Muslims in Denmark, they are, however, never explicitly highlighted in the legislation due to equal treatment.

Of initial interest is the fact that the institutions of the Church of Denmark as well as recognised religious communities are exempt from the *Foundations Act*, which means that rules and regulations regarding articles of association, leadership, accounting and accountability do not apply. The exemption is in effect as long as the institutions and religious communities do not undertake any other tasks beyond their main purpose.

> Bekendtgørelse af lov om fonde og visse foreninger (LBK nr 938 af 20/09/2012)[3]
>
> Kapitel 1
> *Lovens anvendelsesområde*
> § 1. Lovens kapitel 1–12 gælder for fonde, legater, stiftelser og andre selvejende institutioner (fonde).

1 Vinding & Christoffersen 2012, pp. 97 ff.

2 A case in point is U2008.342 H, where an independent group of Roman Catholics argued the unconstitutionality of and violation of international human rights in the current system of state support for the Church of Denmark. Discussed in Vinding & Christoffersen 2012, p. 99.

3 https://www.retsinformation.dk/Forms/R0710.aspx?id=138731, accessed 1 November 2019.

Stk. 2. Loven omfatter ikke:
1) fonde, som er oprettet ved eller i henhold til lov eller ved mellemfolkelig overenskomst mellem Danmark og en anden stat, og som er undergivet tilsyn af en af staterne,
2) fonde, med hvilke en kommune eller region har indgået aftale til opfyldelse af kommunens eller regionens forpligtelser i henhold til lov om social service, såfremt fonden ikke varetager andre opgaver,
3) folkekirkens selvejende institutioner, trossamfund og godkendte uddannelsesinstitutioner, såfremt fonden ikke ud over sit hovedformål varetager andre opgaver.

Also, in the *Act on Corporation Tax*, corresponding to the provisions above, religious communities are exempt from paying taxes. Of significant importance here is, however, the wording that only recognised religious communities are exempt from taxes—not all religious communities.

Bekendtgørelse af selskabsskatteloven (LBK nr 1164 af 06/09/2016)[4]

Skattepligten
§ 3. Undtaget fra skattepligten er:
1) Staten og dens institutioner, jf. dog § 1, stk. 1, nr. 2 d, 2 g, 2 i og 2 j.
2) Regionerne og kommunerne samt regionale og kommunale virksomheder og institutioner, jf. dog stk. 7 og § 1, stk. 1, nr. 2 f og 2 h.
3) Anerkendte trossamfund og kirkelige institutioner, oprettet i tilslutning til disse eller til folkekirken.

However, in the provisions of the 2018 *Act on Religious Communities outside the Church of Denmark* some related issues are addressed, in particular regarding articles of associations and audited accounts of recognised religious communities. As has already been discussed, many religious communities are not recognised and have no intention of seeking recognition.

According to this, members of religious communities may be allowed to deduct on their tax returns the value of gifts, alms and charitable donations. This applies only if the communities are found to be actual religious communities—in either Denmark or other EU countries—and only if the religious community declares the donations to the tax authorites.

4 https://www.retsinformation.dk/Forms/R0710.aspx?id=183480, accessed 1 November 2019.

Bekendtgørelse af lov om påligningen af indkomstskat til staten (ligningsloven) (LBK nr 1162 af 01/09/2016)[5]

§ 8 A. Ved opgørelsen af den skattepligtige indkomst kan fradrages gaver, som det godtgøres, at giveren har ydet til foreninger, stiftelser, institutioner mv., hvis midler anvendes i almenvelgørende eller på anden måde almennyttigt øjemed til fordel for en større kreds af personer. Fradraget kan ikke udgøre mere end et grundbeløb på 14.500 kr. (2010-niveau), som reguleres efter personskattelovens § 20. Endelig er fradrag betinget af, at foreningen m.v. har indberettet indbetalingen til told- og skatteforvaltningen i overensstemmelse med de regler, som er fastsat af skatteministeren i medfør af skattekontrollovens § 8 Æ, stk. 3.
Stk. 2. Fradragsretten efter stk. 1 er betinget af, at foreningen eller det religiøse samfund m.v. er godkendt her i landet eller i et andet EU/EØS-land, hvor det er hjemmehørende, for det kalenderår, hvori donationen gives, jf. stk. 3. Det skal af vedtægter, fundats el.lign. fremgå, at formålet er almenvelgørende, dvs. at midlerne alene kan anvendes til støtte for en videre kreds af personer, som er i økonomisk trang eller har vanskelige økonomiske forhold, eller til et formål, som ud fra en i befolkningen almindeligt herskende opfattelse kan karakteriseres som nyttigt, og som kommer en vis større kreds til gode, eller at der er tale om et trossamfund

The easiest way to establish whether religious communities are in fact religious communities is if the community is recognised under the *Act on Religious Communities outside the Church of Denmark*. If the tax authorities accept this, then this provision of the *Tax Assessment Act* is the single most significant indirect support for religious communities. Exemptions from paying taxes may be of considerable value, too, but this right to deduct donations to charities opens up sources of revenue, which are subsequently exempt from tax. One issue here, however, is that it takes some administration and the proper management of funds and donations to declare the deductions to the authorities, a fact which might add a burden to very small religious communities. Another issue, which in recent years has become more apparent, is that the provision allowing for the deduction from tax of donations to religious communities is of significant benefit to wealthy communities. Since the *Act on Religious Communities outside the Church of Denmark* has made the audited financial records of recognised Islamic cummunities available through the register,

5 https://www.retsinformation.dk/Forms/R0710.aspx?id=183458, accessed 1 November 2019.

it has become evident that for some communities the relative poverty of their members means that the benefit of the exemption is minimal.

A more curious aspect regarding indirect state support for religious communities concerns public debt.

Bekendtgørelse af lov om inddrivelse af gæld til det offentlige (LBK nr 29 af 12/01/2015)[6]

Fordringer, der kan inddrives ved lønindeholdelse, jf. § 10, og fordringer, der kan inddrives ved udpantning, jf. § 11:
1) Stats- og kommuneskatter samt afgifter og ydelser, som ifølge lov tilkommer stat, kommune, kirker, anerkendte trossamfund, offentlige stiftelser eller embeder og bestillinger, herunder skattebeløb, som en indeholdelsespligtig har været forpligtet til at indeholde eller opkræve, samt parafiskale udgifter.
2) Enhver på en fast ejendom hvilende, stadig tilbagevendende eller af en bestemt begivenhed afhængig pengeafgift, som uden særlig vedtagelse går over fra ejer til ejer, og tilkommer stat, kommune, kirker, anerkendte trossamfund, offentlige stiftelser eller embeder og bestillinger, når afgiftens størrelse fastsættes efter faste regler.

In accordance with the *Law on Public Debt Recovery* any legal debt that is owed to a religious community may be collected by withholding salaries. This is, however, somewhat hypothetical as it is unclear which parts of debts owed to religious communities might be considered public and legal.

One case of what might be considered direct support to religious communities concerns the *Executive Order on Distribution of Subsidies for Certain Periodicals and Magazines*.

Bekendtgørelse om distributionstilskud til visse periodiske blade og tidsskrifter (BEK nr 1181 af 02/11/2017)[7]

Kapitel 1
Kriterier for tilskud
§ 1. Der ydes tilskud til distribution i Danmark samt fra Danmark til Færøerne og Grønland til en udgiver af et periodisk blad og tidsskrift, forudsat

6 https://www.retsinformation.dk/forms/r0710.aspx?id=167374, accessed 1 November 2019.
7 https://www.retsinformation.dk/Forms/R0710.aspx?id=194405, accessed 1 November 2019.

at publikationen udkommer med mindst to numre pr. kalenderår og fortrinsvis udgøres af information om:
1) Almennyttige eller almenvelgørende emner, fortrinsvis generel information om samfund og omverden, sociale forhold, sundhed og sygdom.
2) Humanitære organisationers virke.
3) Undervisning og skoleforhold, herunder enkelte fag.
4) Idræt, fortrinsvis information om idrætsgrene og foreningsliv i tilknytning hertil.
5) Kunst og kultur, fortrinsvis information om billedkunst, litteratur, musik, film og teater samt kulturformidling og kulturbevaring.
6) Miljø, fortrinsvis information om naturbevaring og naturforbedring, alternativ energi, miljøbeskyttelse og miljøopretning.
7) Religiøse emner, dvs. blade udgivet af trossamfund, sammenslutninger af trossamfund eller organisationer, der er oprettet af ét eller flere trossamfund eller en kreds af trossamfundsmedlemmer. Ved et trossamfund forstås en organisation eller forening, der er anerkendt eller godkendt som trossamfund af Kirkeministeriet.

According to section 1, "subsidies may be awarded for distribution in Denmark as well as from Denmark to the Faroe Islands and Greenland to a publisher of a periodical magazine and journal, provided that the publication releases at least two issues per calendar year." This is then specified to apply to a number of topics, including number 7, "religious topics, i.e. magazines published by religious communities, associations of religious communities or organisations set up by one or more religious communities or a group of religious community members. A religious community is understood to be an organisation or association that is recognised or approved as a religious community by the Ministry of Ecclesiastical Affairs."

In 2018, of the religious communities supported in publishing magazines the Jewish Society in Denmark received almost 12,000 DKK for its *Jødisk Orientering* (Jewish Orientation) and the Catholic Church in Denmark received more than 200,000 DKK for its *Katolsk Orientering* (Catholic Orientation).[8] However, no Islamic community received—or even, perhaps, applied for—funding to publish anything. This despite that fact that the inspiration for something like 'Muslim Orientation' is obvious.

8 List of magazines supported by 'Bladpuljen,' in 2018. https://slks.dk/fileadmin/user_upload/0_SLKS/Dokumenter/Medier/Mediestoette/Bladpuljen_2018/Bladpuljen_2018.pdf, accessed 1 November 2019.

A final example of viable state support concerns support for signing and interpretation for persons with hearing impairment in the *Executive Order on Activities with indefinite interpretation for people with hearing impairments*.

Bekendtgørelse om aktiviteter med tidsubegrænset tolkning til personer med hørehandicap (BEK nr 945 af 27/07/2010)[9]

I medfør af § 10 i lov nr. 1503 af 27. december 2009 om tolkning til personer med hørehandicap fastsættes:
§ 1. Der ydes ubegrænset tolkning til aktiviteterne nævnt i bilag 1.
§ 2. Bekendtgørelsen træder i kraft den 1. august 2010.
Stk. 2. Samtidig ophæves bekendtgørelse nr. 416 af 21. april 2010 om aktiviteter med tidsubegrænset tolkning til personer med hørehandicap.

The *ratio legis* is that the hearing impaired should be able to participate in activities in community life on an equal footing with other citizens. Section 1 specifies that unlimited interpretation is available to people with hearing impairments as regards the activities mentioned in the appendix to the executive order. One finds mentioned explicitly approved and recognised religious communities, which may have such support for community directed religious activities, such as baptisms, confirmations, weddings, funerals, worship, confirmation preparation and other similar religious acts. Also, with regard to other religious acts, such as the installation of a minister or other religious personnel, support is available for regular work associated with parish council meetings, such as participation in council meetings, in job interviews and other committee meetings.

Folkekirken samt godkendte og anerkendte trossamfund:[10]

Udøvelse af offentlig myndighed med borgerlig retsvirkning
Borgerrettede religiøse handlinger
  Barnedåb, konfirmation, bryllup, begravelse, gudstjeneste, konfirmationsforberedelse og andre tilsvarende religiøse handlinger
Andre religiøse handlinger
  Indsættelse af præst

9 https://www.retsinformation.dk/Forms/R0710.aspx?id=133003, accessed 1 November 2019.

10 https://www.retsinformation.dk/Forms/R0710.aspx?id=133003, accessed 1 November 2019.

Menighedsrådsarbejde
  Deltagelse i menihedsrådsmøder
  Deltagelse i ansættelsessamtaler og andre udvalgsmøder

From this overlooked executive order it may be assumed that Muslims with hearing impairments may get state support for signing or interpretation when participating in religious activities, mosques' organisational work or even other committee meetings as part of the work associated with running the Islamic religious community. Whether they actually apply for and get such support is unclear.

CHAPTER 4

Islamic Community

In Denmark, there is no explicit legal framework to establish, support or encourage the Islamic community as such. There are a number of general legal provisions applying to all recognised religious communities and indirect support that of course applies to Islamic communities, too. Nevertheless, there is no explicit legal establishment of Islamic communities, like France's *Conseil français du culte musulman* or Austria's *Islamgesetz* of 2015, which can be traced back to 1912. By way of comparison, it is important to stress that the Danish state does not explicitly establish, support or encourage any other religious communities, beyond the Church of Denmark.

There are a number of umbrella or uniting initiatives, such as *Dansk Islamisk Union* (the Danish Islamic Union), *Islamisk Trossamfund* (the Islamic Faith Society) and *Det Danske Islamiske Råd* (the Danish Islamic Council), but none of them has been able to claim to speak on behalf of all or even a majority of Muslims in Denmark.

Currently, there are no initiatives to establish a formal, public agenda or conversation with Muslims in Denmark, compared to, for example, the *Deutsche Islamkonferenz*, or to set up a nationally representative institution, such as the French council. Jonathan Laurence argues in his *Emancipation of Muslims in Europe* that there is a correlation between emancipation and legal rights, on the one hand, and the establishment of representative institutions, on the other. Where Muslims have defunct or non-functional organisational representation at the national level, they enjoy fewer rights, have fewer options and experience a greater degree of discrimination (Laurence, 2012). Arguably, Danish Muslims might very well be a case in point to support such an argument.

The only thing that came close to a national ambition on the part of Muslims in engaging state and government in dialogue is worth highlighting: a series of three meetings held on 30 November 2004, 20 September 2005 and 13 February 2006 at the initiative of the then Prime Minister, Anders Fogh Rasmussen. The Ministry and Office of the Prime Minister invited a number of spokesmen, representatives, leading figures and politicians to informal talks at the official residence, Marienborg. Nothing significant came of these meetings, but their overall agendas were published, and they covered issues concerning integration, terrorism, Islamic extremism and inter-religious dialogue. As remains clear from the press releases and the comments coming from these meetings, the agenda was set and the meetings were held entirely at the discretion of the Office of the Prime Minister, with little or perhaps no ambition for a political outcome to further the rights and conditions of the Islamic community in Denmark.[1]

1 On Muslim organisations in Denmark and deliberations with the state see, further, Vinding 2013, pp. 129–133.

CHAPTER 5

Muslims in Integration Law

As with most other European countries, through the second half of the 20th and first decades of the 21st centuries, Denmark has seen a significantly increasing presence of Muslims and other immigrants from the Muslim majority world as well as Eastern Europe and South-East Asia. Similar to other European countries, but perhaps to a greater degree, the Danish government decided to tighten immigration and integration legislation in the 21st century and accelerated this significantly after the migration crisis of 2015 and 2016. The legislation enacted and amended after this crisis constitutes the bulk of legal documents discussed in this chapter.

5.1 Legal Residence for Religious Personnel

The *Aliens Act* regulates much of the legal framework for legally entering Denmark and obtaining permits to work and stay. This law applies generally but has recently been subject to much political debate and legal revision due to recent trends in anti-immigration sentiments, increased awareness of migrants and refugees as well as an increasing national populism.

Following the recent trends of increased migration and the political reactions to restrict legal residency, right to stay and work permits, the *Aliens Act* has been significantly amended (LBK 1117, 2 October 2017). It includes several new and very strict conditions, especially regarding rules for expulsion, control across different public registries, limitations on open-ended residence permits, rescinding student visas if students take up work, and much stricter rules on applying for residence permits. In addition, there is no longer an unlimited right to a residence permit in order to bring about a family reunion with a view in particular to marriages. If a marriage appears to be forced or a marriage of convenience entered into in order to obtain a residence permit, the permit will not be granted and the marriage will not be recognised. Subject to ECHR Articles 8 and 12 and the UN conventions, the *Udlændingestyrelsen* (Danish Immigration Service) must verify the existence of all the legal conditions. The result of the new rules is that the number of family reunions among immigrants is reduced. Also, the number of forced marriages of young immigrant women has been reduced in recent years.

The strict regime of the consecutive governments regarding immigrants, asylum seekers and Muslims has been criticised by opposition parties. Such vocal criticism peaked after then Minister for Immigration, Integration and Housing, Inger Støjberg, who was quite popular but controversial, directed the immigration authorities to separate 27 couples in the Danish asylum system where one of the parties—usually the bride—was under age. One such young Syrian couple, the husband aged 26 and the wife 17 and pregnant, were separated by authorities in 2016. The minister's order was criticised by the Ombudsman, the separations were deemed illegal by the courts and the couple was granted compensation.

While the law is developing into quite a complex and detailed legal instrument—as is seen in the next sections—it still regulates a number of aspects that concern religious personel in general, and de facto has great significance for visiting preachers, imams and other religious leaders in Muslim communities.

Bekendtgørelse af udlændingeloven (LBK nr 1117 af 02/10/2017)[1]

§ 9f
[…]
Der kan efter ansøgning gives opholdstilladelse til
1) en udlænding, der her i landet skal virke som religiøs forkynder,
2) en udlænding, der her i landet skal virke som missionær, eller
3) en udlænding, der her i landet skal virke inden for et religiøst ordenssamfund.
Stk. 2. Opholdstilladelse efter stk. 1 skal betinges af, at udlændingen godtgør at have tilknytning til folkekirken eller et anerkendt eller godkendt trossamfund her i landet. Meddelelse af opholdstilladelse efter stk. 1 er betinget af, at antallet af udlændinge med opholdstilladelse efter stk. 1 inden for trossamfundet står i rimeligt forhold til trossamfundets størrelse.
Stk. 3. Opholdstilladelse efter stk. 1 skal betinges af, at udlændingen godtgør at have en relevant baggrund eller uddannelse for at virke som religiøs forkynder eller missionær eller inden for et religiøst ordenssamfund.
Stk. 4. Opholdstilladelse efter stk. 1 skal betinges af, at udlændingen underskriver en løfteerklæring om, at den pågældende i sit virke vil overholde dansk lovgivning.
Stk. 5. Forlængelse af opholdstilladelse efter stk. 1 skal betinges af, at ansøgeren inden 6 måneder efter meddelelsen af opholdstilladelsen har

1 https://www.retsinformation.dk/Forms/R0710.aspx?id=194003, accessed 1 November 2019.

bestået en prøve i dansk på A1-minus-niveau, jf. bekendtgørelse nr. 981 af 28. juni 2016 om danskuddannelse til voksne udlændinge m.fl., og danske samfundsforhold. Udlændinge- og integrationsministeren fastsætter regler om prøven, herunder regler om, hvornår prøven anses for bestået, frist for aflæggelse og beståelse af prøven, om udpegning af prøveafholdere, betingelser for at deltage i prøven, opkrævning af gebyr for at deltage i prøven, klagefrister og prøvens indhold og gennemførelse m.v.

Stk. 6. Forlængelse af opholdstilladelse efter stk. 1 skal endvidere betinges af, at ansøgeren inden 6 måneder efter meddelelse af opholdstilladelse har gennemført et kursus i dansk familieret, frihed og folkestyre, der er etableret af udlændinge- og integrationsministeren. Det påhviler ansøgeren inden for de 6 måneder at fremlægge dokumentation herfor. Fristen på 6 måneder kan efter ansøgning forlænges ved lovligt forfald. 1. og 2. pkt. finder ikke anvendelse, hvis ansøgeren fritages for at deltage i kurset, fordi den pågældende har et tilsvarende kendskab til dansk familieret, frihed og folkestyre.

Stk. 7. Opholdstilladelse efter stk. 1 skal betinges af, at udlændingen og personer, der meddeles opholdstilladelse som følge af familiemæssig tilknytning til udlændingen, ikke modtager offentlig hjælp til forsørgelse under opholdet her i landet.

Stk. 8. Opholdstilladelse efter stk. 1 kan ikke meddeles, hvis der er grund til at antage, at udlændingen vil udgøre en trussel mod den offentlige tryghed, den offentlige orden, sundheden, sædeligheden eller andres rettigheder og pligter.

Stk. 9. Ansøgning om opholdstilladelse efter stk. 1 kan kun indgives her i landet, hvis udlændingen har lovligt ophold i medfør af §§ 1–3 a, § 4 b eller § 5, stk. 2, i medfør af EU-reglerne, jf. § 6, eller en opholdstilladelse efter §§ 7–9 f, 9 i–9 n eller 9 p, og hvis ingen særlige grunde taler herimod. Hvis udlændingen ikke har lovligt ophold, har fået fastsat en udrejsefrist eller har en anden ansøgning om opholdstilladelse under behandling, kan ansøgning om opholdstilladelse efter stk. 1 ikke indgives her i landet. En ansøgning om forlængelse af en opholdstilladelse, der er meddelt efter stk. 1, skal indgives før tilladelsens udløb, for at udlændingen kan anses for at have lovligt ophold, jf. 1. pkt.

Stk. 10. Udlændinge- og integrationsministeren fastsætter efter aftale med kirkeministeren nærmere regler om kurset i dansk familieret, frihed og folkestyre, herunder regler om kursets indhold, lovligt forfald, fritagelse for at deltage i kurset, ansøgningsproceduren og opkrævning af gebyr for at deltage i kurset, jf. stk. 6.

Section 9f of the *Aliens Act* regulates the rights to import into Denmark religious preachers, religious missionaries or personnel working with religious orders on temporary residence permits. Such permits are contingent upon a long list of factors, explained in sections 1 to 10. Temporary residence permits for religious personel are possible if the religious community is recognised and its size warrants the issue of one (section 2). Also, there are requirements that the religious person in question is qualified (section 3), promises to abide by Danish law (section 4), receives no public benefits (section 7), has filed no other application to stay (section 9), that there is no reason to suspect any threat to public safety, order, health or decency, and that the person is not in violation of the rights and duties of others (section 8). If such people want to extend their stay, they must pass a Danish language exam (section 5). Finally, and most significantly, all religious personel must now participate in a mandatory course on Danish family law, freedom and democracy (sections 6 and 10). The Minister for Aliens and Immigration together with the Minister for Ecclesiastical Affairs is charged with designing the content and rules for participation and exemption, as well as the application for and the fees for the course.

The mandatory course on Danish family law, freedom and democracy was vociferously criticised by the Muslim communities in Denmark, in particular the Danish Muslim Union, in a hearing response of 29 October 2016, as they saw the course as directed at Muslim preachers, only thinly veiled by general statements. The assumption that guest preachers would work to undermine Danish values, freedoms and rights is undocumented and the amendment works to alienate Muslims. Rather than building on factual or proportional considerations, the amendment is motivated by ideology, "and will contribute to further polarisation and stigmatisation of Muslims and Islam in society."[2]

The particular case of the so-called *Ankara agreement* is worth mentioning as it reflects the pragmatic negotiations of the 1960s, 1970s and 1980s regarding Turkish nationals and residents. The *Association Agreement with Turkey* between the European Economic Community and Turkey, originally dated 1964, but with an important amendment of 1980, regulates Turkish religious confessors and missionaries.[3] It specifies that economically active Turkish nationals may have special rights to continue their legal residence in Denmark although the basis for their original residence and work permit no

2 Dansk Muslimsk Union, "Baggrunden for lovforslaget stærkt bekymrende," Høringssvar 29 October 2016.

3 https://www.nyidanmark.dk/da/Ord-og-begreber/F%C3%A6lles/Associeringsaftalen-med-Tyrkiet, accessed 1 November 2019.

longer exists. This also applies to family members of Turkish nationals, regardless of the nationality of the family members. The following quotation is from the Danish Immigration Service's commentary on the agreement.[4]

> Da religiøse forkyndere, der skal forkynde det religiøse budskab som præst, imam eller lignende, må anses som værende arbejdstagere, idet de skal arbejde for trossamfundet, er de materielle vilkår for den første indrejse for tyrkiske statsborgere, der agter at gøre brug af denne frihed her i landet, omfattet [...] Opholdstilladelse med henblik på at virke inden for et religiøst ordenssamfund kan gives, hvis udlændingen kan fremlægge dokumentation for, at han/hun skal virke inden for et religiøst ordenssamfund. Der tænkes her på nonner og munke, som traditionelt har et religiøst virke internt i et ordenssamfund. Folkekirken eller et anerkendt eller godkendt trossamfund skal erklære over for Udlændingestyrelsen, at ordenssamfundet er oprettet af og/eller virker inden for trossamfundet.
> For sådanne missionærer kan der normalt meddeles opholdstilladelse for 1 år med mulighed for forlængelse for 1 år ad gangen i sammenlagt højst 3 år.
>
> Familiemedlemmer
> En udenlandsk religiøs forkynder, missionær eller person, der skal virke inden for et religiøst ordenssamfund, har ikke krav på at få sin familie med til Danmark. Hvis opholdstilladelsen kan gives eller forlænges til et ophold på 3 år eller mere, kan en ægtefælle, registreret partner eller fast samlever samt hjemmeboende børn under 18 dog også få opholdstilladelse. Det er i givet fald en betingelse, at familien kan forsørge sig selv og skal bo samlet her i Danmark. Får en ægtefælle, registreret partner eller samlever opholdstilladelse, vil han eller hun have ret til at arbejde, så længe tilladelsen er gyldig.

4 "Agreement creating an association between the European Economic Community and Turkey," signed in Ankara on 12 September 1963 and entered into force on 1 December 1964, https://www.europarl.europa.eu/delegations/en/d-tr/documents/eu-texts, accessed 1 February 2020.

5.2 Public Sanction List against Religious 'Hate Preachers'

A similar step in the 'ideological' direction, and clearly part of the political regime of tightening and limiting immigration, the *Aliens Act* was amended in December 2016, this time to limit a certain number of named religious preachers from outside the EU entering Denmark, because their preaching and opinions are seen as so-called hate speech. The amendment establishes a public list of such named religious preachers barred from entry and a confidential watchlist of potential names for the list.

L 48 Forslag til lov om ændring af udlændingeloven.
(Indførelse af en offentlig sanktionsliste over udenlandske religiøse forkyndere m.fl., som kan udelukkes fra at indrejse).[5]

Kapitel 5—Liste over udenlandske religiøse forkyndere m.fl., som kan udelukkes fra at indrejse
§ 29 c. En udlænding kan optages på en liste, hvis udlændingen virker som religiøs forkynder eller på anden måde udbreder en religion eller tro og hensynet til den offentlige orden i Danmark tilsiger, at udlændingen ikke bør have ophold her i landet. Optagelse på listen sker for 2 år og kan forlænges med 2 år ad gangen. En udlænding, som er omfattet af EU-reglerne, jf. § 2, stk. 3, eller har opholdstilladelse her i landet, kan ikke optages på listen.
Stk. 2. Ved afgørelse om optagelse af en udlænding på den liste, der er nævnt i stk. 1, finder forvaltningslovens § 19 ikke anvendelse.
Stk. 3. Optagelse af en udlænding på den liste, der er nævnt i stk. 1, optages som meddelelse i Statstidende. Optagelse af en udlænding på listen gælder fra tidspunktet for optagelse af meddelelse herom i Statstidende, medmindre optagelse på listen forud for dette tidspunkt er meddelt den pågældende udlænding.
Stk. 4. Den liste, der er nævnt i stk. 1, kan offentliggøres med oplysninger om navn, nationalitet, fødselsdato og opholdsland og med ansigtsfoto.
Stk. 5. Efter anmodning fra udlændingen genoptager Udlændingestyrelsen sagen om at optage udlændingen på den liste, der er nævnt i stk. 1. Ansøgning om genoptagelse har ikke opsættende virkning.

5 "L48, Forslag til lov om ændring af udlændingeloven," http://www.ft.dk/samling/20161/lovforslag/L48/som_vedtaget.htm, accessed 1 November 2019.

The political reason for this amendment was the abovementioned political compromise and agreement in principle of 31 May 2016 between the government, the Social Democrats, the Danish People's Party and the Conservative Party to limit religious preachers, in part by not allowing them to enter Denmark. They agreed that such travelling 'hate preachers' were a threat to public order in Denmark, and that they would be denied visas and entry at the Danish border. However, this was more easily agreed and enacted than actually done, as political opposition, lawyers and scholars have criticized the bill.

First and foremost, preachers who came from other EU countries could not be denied visas or entry. Secondly, many of the worst of such 'hate preachers, who were actually calling for Jihad or recruiting for ISIS were already on the international terrorist lists or other international criminal watchlists. Thirdly, much of the 'hate' and public disorder that is feared politically may just as well come from Danish residents and citizens or via the internet or other media.

Nevertheless, the Ministry of Immigration and Integration was charged with collecting information on foreign religious preachers through the internet or the reports of other authorities, and going through statements, videos and other public or private information. In order to be on the list, the individual must have displayed conduct—in speech or action—which gives reason to believe that they would pose a threat to public order in Denmark if they were allowed to enter. Also, there must be a certain likelihood that the foreigner in question will attempt to enter Denmark. This process is entirely administrative and does not require judicial oversight.[6]

The kind of speech or actions that would make an individual likely to be put on the list is explored in the preparatory drafting text of the amendment. This includes statements abroad that would be punishable if they had been made in Denmark; public incitement to crimes or one of the offences referred to in the Criminal Code, such as crimes against public order or state security and violations of the Constitution or encouragemet to terrorism; and those who publicly mock or deride anything in this country's legally existing religious communities' religious teachings or worship, cf. section 140 of the Criminal Code.

Further included are statements made abroad which, by their content, undermine and counteract the principles of democracy and respect for human rights on which Danish society is based. These include statements that do not respect basic principles such as equality of race, gender, sexuality, religion or freedom of speech.

6 "L48, Forslag til lov om ændring af udlændingeloven," lovforslag som fremsat med forarbejder, https://www.ft.dk/samling/20161/lovforslag/L48/som_fremsat.htm, accessed 1 November 2019.

The zeal and creativity of lawmakers in coming up with possible examples of what such speech or actions might be leaves little to the imagination or source of inspiration for the legislators. They have prepared examples of speech and behaviour that would generally imply that public policy considerations in Denmark indicate that a religious preacher should not have residence in the country, and they then mention the following:[7]

- It will include ... statements whereby the person expresses support and seeks to endorse the establishment of Caliphate rule or dictatorship in the country, to the extent that the statements are of a such an extreme nature that they give reason to believe that the person in question would pose a threat to public policy in Denmark if they were allowed to enter this country.
- In connection with the mention of a bomb attack in a magazine, a foreign religious preacher calls for more powerful and dangerous means to be used on future occasions. (Section 136 (1) of the Criminal Code and U.1938.407 Ø).
- A foreign religious preacher supports explicitly on a website a specific terrorist attack perpetrated by suicide bombers.
- A foreign religious preacher states in a post on a website that people of a particular religion generally commit serious crimes such as rape, mistreatment and murder (Penal Code § 266 b and U.2014.73.V).
- A foreign religious preacher systematically, intensively and persistently argues in study circles and on websites for the introduction of a different form of government from democracy in Europe, including Denmark.

Interestingly enough, these 'imagined examples' look like caricatures of something that would be associated with Islamic hate preachers or terrorists, and this seems to have satisfied the political need to demonstrate a hard line. Nevertheless, the examples listed by the ministerial jurists in paranthesis tell another surprising story. While the prose goes in one direction, the two legal cases mentioned show something else. The first, U.1938.407Ø, which is mentioned in relation to the bombing of a magazine and thus echoing the 7 January 2015 *Charlie Hebdo* attack, actually concerns an editor who in 1938 was charged, because of

7 "L48, Forslag til lov om ændring af udlændingeloven," lovforslag som fremsat med forarbejder, https://www.ft.dk/samling/20161/lovforslag/L48/som_fremsat.htm, accessed 1 November 2019.

an article about a bomb attack on the defence minister's villa, where he indirectly called for the use of more powerful bombs to be used against ministers. Such an example, especially in the context of World War II, speaks to political right-wing rather than religious motives. The other case referred to, U.2014.73V, in a finding that 'a particular religion generally commits serious crimes such as rape, mistreatment and murder,' actually concerned hate speech directed against Muslims. The Higher Court convicted a woman of incitement to hatred and hate speech for a statement on a website. In her statement she wrote that Muslim men raped and killed their daughters based on defective culture and religion. To put it clearly, the legislative ambition relates to one imagined scenario where Muslims are assumed to be hate preachers, but the Danish case law paints a picture of Danish right-wing hate speech.

Ultimately, the first version of the list was revealed on 1 May 2017 and, not surprisingly, the ambition of sending political signals by way of legislation prevailed.[8] All but one were, not surprisingly, Islamic leaders or scholars. The only one clearly not Muslim was Terry Jones, infamous for burning the Quran in Florida. The first list included six names, which then grew through the following years to include a total of 19 names.[9] Five have also been removed, including Salman Alodah who, as a critic of the Saudi regime and a dissident, was awaiting execution in Saudi Arabia. Whether he was put on the list to begin with by mistake and then removed, or whether he was removed from the list because, as a prisoner in Saudi Arabia, he was unlikely to seek entry into Denmark, is difficult to know. The fact of the matter remains that it is utterly unclear and gravely problematic how this list is managed and maintained.

Not only have the tight regulations and legislation attracted significant criticism, but the sanctions list of hate preachers has been one of the most vociferously criticised. During the hearing process, the Council of the Danish Bar and Law Society criticised the administrative nature of the powers under the amendment, which means that the foreign preacher is not privy to the details of his own case or the decision regarding it.[10] They found that the amendment was inadvisable from a rule of law perspective and that it should be reconsidered. It was not.

8 https://www.dr.dk/nyheder/indland/stoejberg-liste-over-hadpraedikanter-er-ikke-bare-symbolpolitik, accessed 1 November 2019.

9 https://www.nyidanmark.dk/da/Ord-og-begreber/US/Religi%C3%B8se-forkyndere/Religi%C3%B8se-forkyndere-med-indrejseforbud/?anchor=7C5D2D143D284E4EB2829BA5F0F04837&callbackItem=C6E4B3675A6C4C4B9F3B70C734981907&callbackAnchor=C6E4B3675A6C4C4B9F3B70C734981907, accessed 1 November 2019.

10 Advokatrådet, "Høringssvar til L48," 1 November 2016.

Most vocal, however, was the *Retspolitisk Forening* (Legal Political Association), which advocates for the rule of law and for civil, social and democratic rights. It concluded that the amendment thus seemed to be yet another example of almost content-empty token legislation, adding to the list of attemps to make difficult the constitutionally guaranteed freedom of religion of religious preachers from the Islamic faith community. All things considered, they argued, the amendment is unlikely to have any effect and should not be proposed.[11]

5.3 Ceremonies Celebrating New Citizens

Following the trend explored above of taking a hard line against religious extremism thought to be associated with Islam and legislating based on such assumption, a final example regarding Muslims and immigration law must be highlighted. The fervour of the previous government in demonstrating Danishness and acting against Islam came together in a 2018 amendment to the *Law on Danish Citizenship*, which delegates to the Minister for Immigation and Integration the power to make it mandatory that new citizens shake hands with a representative of the authorities.[12] The less than implicit assumption is that fundamentalist Muslims might not want to shake the hands of people of the opposite sex and thus would not participate in the ceremony.

In its reasoning and drafting comments, the Government argues that "it is crucial for a society like the Danish to meet each other in a proper way with trust and respect" (p. 2), and that "it is an expression of a basic Danish value and cultural norm that you show respect when you meet one another by exchanging handshakes with one another" (p. 2). As part of a constitutional ceremony, citizens-to-be are to "meet face-to-face with the other participants and exchange handshakes with the other participants without gloves, palm to palm, to celebrate. This, in effect, marks the moment in the participants' lives where they become Danish citizens" (p. 6). Anticipating and assessing the constitutionality of the handshakes, the drafting comments argue that "a refusal to shake hands with representatives of the authorities in itself can be considered

11 Retspolitisk Forening, "Høringssvar til L48," 1 November 2016.

12 "L80, Forslag til Lov om ændring af lov om dansk indfødsret og lov om danskuddannelse til voksne udlændinge m.fl. (Henlæggelse til kommunalbestyrelserne af grundlovsceremonier, forhøjelse af gebyr for ansøgning om dansk indfødsret ved naturalisation samt fastsættelse af nærmere regler om udlændinges fravær i undervisning i dansk m.v.)," https://www.ft.dk/samling/20181/lovforslag/L80/som_fremsat.htm, accessed 1 November 2019.

to be covered by section 67 of the Constitution as part of worship," but that "it should be noted that in Denmark, a handshake is a common and traditional form of greeting, showing respect for the people you greet. Respect for each other can be regarded as a fundamental social value, and this is expressed in Denmark, among other things, in a handshake. On this basis, it is considered that the condition pursues a legitimate purpose" (p. 9).

> Lovforslaget har til formål at henlægge den ceremonielle underskrivning af at ville overholde grundloven m.v. til kommunalbestyrelserne. I den forbindelse indeholder lovforslaget et forslag om at bemyndige udlændinge- og integrationsministeren til at fastsætte nærmere regler om afholdelsen af disse ceremonier. Det er en betingelse for optagelse på et lovforslag om indfødsrets meddelelse, at ansøgeren lover troskab og loyalitet over for Danmark og det danske samfund og erklærer at ville overholde dansk lovgivning, herunder Danmarks Riges Grundlov, og respektere grundlæggende danske værdier og retsprincipper, herunder det danske demokrati. Dette sker i praksis i forbindelse med ansøgningens indgivelse.
> Regeringen mener, at det er afgørende for et samfund som det danske, at man møder hinanden på en ordentlig måde med tillid og respekt. Det er således udtryk for en grundlæggende dansk værdi og kulturnorm, at man udviser respekt, når man møder hinanden, herunder myndighedsrepræsentanter ved offentlige ceremonier, ved at udveksle håndtryk med hinanden. Det er således efter regeringens opfattelse ikke foreneligt med grundlæggende danske værdier eller respekten for vores fælleskab og kulturnormer, hvis en ansøger om dansk indfødsret ved naturalisation under en grundlovsceremoni afviser at give hånd til repræsentanter fra kommunen.[13]
> [...]
>
> Den foreslåede bemyndigelse vil blive anvendt til bl.a. at fastsætte nærmere regler om afviklingen af ceremonierne, således at der sikres en ensartethed og tilstrækkelig højtidelighed ved ceremonierne. Det vil inden for disse regler være op til de enkelte kommunalbestyrelser at tilrettelægge, hvornår og hvordan de ceremonielle begivenheder skal finde sted. Det er herunder hensigten, at udlændinge- og integrationsministeren vil

13 "L80, Forslag til Lov om ændring af lov om dansk indfødsret og lov om danskuddannelse til voksne udlændinge m.fl.," p. 2, https://www.ft.dk/samling/20181/lovforslag/L80/som_fremsat.htm, accessed 1 November 2019.

> anvende bestemmelsen til at fastsætte krav om, at en eller flere repræsentanter fra kommunen i forbindelse med ceremonien mødes ansigt til ansigt med deltagerne og udveksler et håndtryk med deltagerne uden handske håndflade mod håndflade for at højtideligholde og helt konkret markere det øjeblik i deltagernes liv, hvor de bliver danske statsborgere. Med afsæt i en grundlæggende dansk kulturnorm, som håndtrykket efter regeringens opfattelse er udtryk for, vil ansøgeren samtidig ved denne symbolske handling udtrykke den særlige respekt for det danske samfund, som efter regeringens opfattelse bør være forbundet med det at blive tildelt dansk statsborgerskab. Samtidig vil vedkommende symbolsk signalere, at vedkommende har taget det danske samfund og danske værdier til sig. Repræsentanterne fra kommunen skal ikke tiltvinge sig et håndtryk, såfremt ansøgeren ikke ønsker at give et håndtryk.[14]
> [...]
>
> I det omfang en afvisning af at ville give hånd til repræsentanter fra myndighederne i sig selv kan anses for at være omfattet af grundlovens § 67 som en del af gudsdyrkelse, bemærkes, at i Danmark er håndtrykket en almindelig og traditionel hilseform, hvorved man viser respekt for de personer, man hilser på. Det kan anses som en grundlæggende samfundsværdi, at man udviser respekt over for hinanden, og dette udtrykkes i Danmark bl.a. ved håndtrykket. Det vurderes på den baggrund, at betingelsen forfølger et legitimt formål.[15]

By themselves, the government's arguments in proposing the amendment are problematic. It seems to cater to populist notions of national romanticism and anti-Muslim sentiments, which are seen elsewhere across Europe.[16] As such, it demonstrates a remarkable willingness to challenge the limits of the Constitution, merely for the purpose of making a symbolic political point. The lawmaking creativity and skewed ingenuity of the government's arguments take it from considering meeting each other with respect to shaking hands to insist on a mandatory handshake and considering it a legitimate purpose to do so even

14 "L80, Forslag til Lov om ændring af lov om dansk indfødsret og lov om danskuddannelse til voksne udlændinge m.fl.," p. 6, https://www.ft.dk/samling/20181/lovforslag/L80/som_fremsat.htm, accessed 1 November 2019.

15 "L80, Forslag til Lov om ændring af lov om dansk indfødsret og lov om danskuddannelse til voksne udlændinge m.fl.," pp. 8–9, https://www.ft.dk/samling/20181/lovforslag/L80/som_fremsat.htm, accessed 1 November 2019.

16 E.g., Marzouki, N., McDonnell, D., & Roy, O., *Saving the people: How populists hijack religion* (London: Hurst, 2016).

if it violates religious freedom. Through a political performative speech act, the government is equally conjuring up the handshake as core social value, a basic Danish value and cultural norm while at the same time assuming without any established basis that Muslims would be against this.

Again, not surprisingly, such an amendment was met with vociferous criticism, not just from Muslims, but also from other parts of society. The Catholic Church in Denmark criticized the disproportionate and biased logic in putting the citizenship at risk over something as banal as a handshake, and that it might mean that some men would not grant their wives the opportunity to gain Danish citizenship and rights because of this. And, they note, that despite the creativity of the draft, Parliament should not knowingly limit citizenship because of a benign religious practice when no threat to public order or equally grave concen can be established.[17] The Catholic Church sees this as illiberal thought control and a kind of censorship that is unbecoming of Danish tradition and against the spirit of the Constitution. It remains confident that the courts will establish whether such practice is in accordance with the constitutional freedoms and the European Convention on Human Rights.

---

17 *Den Katolske Kirke i Danmark*, "Høringssvar til L80", 1 October 2018.

CHAPTER 6

Mosques and Prayer Houses

Mosques are increasingly becoming a part of the Danish cityscape, and the last few years have seen a growth in major purpose-built mosques in Copenhagen, as well as more and more local mosques throughout Denmark. Local municipal authorities retain the power to regulate the building of new religious buildings generally, including mosques. As Brian Arly Jacobensen[1] has argued, religious buildings and in particular mosques do not necessarily harmonise well with existing housing or district plans. According to the *Planning Act* (*2013*),[2] the municipalities must approve housing or district building plans, and when it comes to mosques politics begins to play a role. Political questions and public concerns are not uncommon in this regard, and challenges whether calls to prayer are considered noise, if minarets are beyond the scope of local planning and who is funding the mosques. These reflect not just political agendas, but a number of documented returning issues that are, amongst others, evidenced recently through the Registry of Religious Communities.

6.1 Proposals to Ban Minarets and Mosques

While there is no legislation that explicitly addresses or limits the building of mosques or Muslim prayer houses, this is not for lack of trying on the part of the Danish People's Party. In recent years, they have put forward several proposals for a parliamentary resolution on this issue. One example will suffice.

Beslutningsforslag nr. B 15[3]
Fremsat den 25. oktober 2016 af Martin Henriksen (DF), Kristian Thulesen Dahl (DF), Søren Espersen (DF), Marie Krarup (DF), Christian Langballe (DF), Merete Dea Larsen (DF), Peter Kofod Poulsen (DF) og Peter Skaarup (DF)

---

1 Jacobsen 2015, "Hellige bygninger på grænsefladen i dansk kommunalpolitik," RVT 62 (2015), pp. 91–105.

2 Bekendtgørelse af lov om planlægning 2013 Bekendtgørelse af lov om planlægning, LBK nr. 587 af 27/05/2013.

3 Beslutningsforslag nr. B 15 Folketinget 2016–2017, https://www.ft.dk/samling/20161/beslutningsforslag/B15/som_fremsat.htm, accessed 1 November 2019.

Forslag til folketingsbeslutning om forbud mod minareter
Folketinget pålægger regeringen i indeværende folketingsår at fremsætte lovforslag om et forbud mod at opføre minareter ved moskeer i Danmark.

This proposal for a parliamentary resolution requires that Parliament should direct the government to draft a bill banning the erection of minarets at mosques in Denmark. Of course, this echoes a European debate after the 2009 Swiss minaret referendum, but in presenting the proposal the Danish People's Party argue that:

> Visible and distinctive Islamic symbols contribute negatively to social development by emphasising the differences between Muslims and Danes, just as these symbols are also impeding the integration of Muslims into Denmark. Against this background, the Danish People's Party wants to prohibit the construction of minarets at mosques in Denmark. The Danish People's Party prefers a total ban on building mosques and also wants to prevent foreign donations financing the construction of religious and cultural symbols related to Islam.[4]

While such a premise is vociferously and widely contested, and the proposal was voted down by every other party in Parliament, the proposal itself reveals its biased and unfounded view of Islam and Muslims. "As religion and ideology, Islam is a disruptive element in Denmark. The Danish People's Party is watching with increasing concern the growing Islamisation of society ..." With such a statement there can be little doubt that the Danish People's Party is seriously not interested in the integration of Islam and Muslims into Danish society.

Arguably, this is the minority opinion of one right-wing party in Denmark. However, during the parliamentary debate that followed this proposal, the then Minister of Immigration and Integration, Inger Støjberg, did in fact share much of the sentiment in the proposal, despite pointing to the fact that the municipalities, rather than government and Parliament, have jurisdiction in the matter of urban planning, housing and zoning. The Minister hardly seemed to miss a chance to equate Islam and Muslim symbols with parallel societies, and thus voicing thinly veiled blame on them for dividing Denmark, while ironically her public statements and actions furthered that exact purpose. She said:

4 "Beslutningsforslag nr. B 15 Folketinget 2016–2017," https://www.ft.dk/samling/20161/beslutningsforslag/B15/som_fremsat.htm, accessed 1 November 2019, author's translation.

> As a rule, it is the municipal council that regulates local planning, which means that it goes through a local democratic process. I have confidence that local politicians will make the right decisions about whether religious buildings may be built, including eg. minarets, and what requirements must be met in that regard.
>
> At the same time, I would also strongly urge religious communities to show consideration to the surrounding community through the specific construction of religious buildings. Against this background, the government is against imposing a ban on the construction of minarets and thus rejects the motion for a resolution.
>
> That being said, I would like to stress that the government fully shares the view evident from the comments on the proposal for a resolution, namely that there is an increasing need to dispute the symbols that are contributing to dividing Denmark. We agree that it is deeply problematic when religious environments close around themselves and parallel societies develop.[5]

A similar case regarding mosques concerns the proposal for a parliamentary resolution on legally banning a specific mosque in Denmark.

> B 14 Forslag til folketingsbeslutning om forbud mod Masjid Al-Faruq-moskeen på Nørrebro.[6]
> Fremsat den 4. oktober 2018 af Martin Henriksen (DF), Alex Ahrendtsen (DF), Kristian Thulesen Dahl (DF), Karina Due (DF), Christian Langballe (DF) og Peter Skaarup (DF)
>
> Folketinget pålægger regeringen at afsøge det juridiske grundlag for at forbyde og lukke Masjid Al-Faruq-moskeen på Nørrebro.

This proposal seeks to commit Parliament to directing the government to explore the legal basis for banning and closing the Masjid Al-Faruq mosque in Nørrebro, in Copenhagen. This proposal was motivated by the fact that one imam from the mosque was being indicted on charges of promoting hate against Jews, charges of which he was later convicted. However, the proposal

---

5 Støjberg remarks regarding "Beslutningsforslag nr. B 15 Folketinget 2016–2017," https://www.ft.dk/samling/20161/beslutningsforslag/B15/BEH1-43/forhandling.htm#t68924C542233449782137DDB3807CA3Atab1, accessed 1 November 2019, author's translation.

6 https://www.ft.dk/samling/20181/beslutningsforslag/b14/index.htm, accessed 1 November 2019.

singles out one mosque and proposes to direct parliamentary and administrative powers to banning and closing it. While biased and utterly unsuccessful in Parliament, this proposal also violates the core principles of the rule of law, namely that judicial power rests with the judiciary—under Article 3 of the Consitution—which is understood to limit the powers of Parliament to legislate on individual issues. According to the Ministry of Justice's own guide to quality of law, the legislature should demonstrate great restraint in individual and concrete issues as opposed to issues of principle. One of the common principles of the rule of law in this regard is that such issues should be dealt with by the administration or the courts on the basis of general rules of law enacted by the legislature.[7] Nevertheless, the Danish People's Party has shown surprisingly little regard for this principle.

6.2 Proposal to Ban Prayer Rooms[8]

A final case and a recent theme in Denmark is the question of the right to worship and to have prayer rooms in public schools and at universities. There is no explicit right to a space or room for prayer, and studies show that they are not common. Ten out of 37 universities and university colleges have facilities for prayer. Of 1,261 schools and similar institutions, 27 have prayer rooms or similar facilities. In addition, an unknown number of institutions make facilities available ad hoc, and usually agreeable and reasonable solutions are found.

However, controversy surfaced in January 2017, when the Danish People's Party in a proposal for a resolution of Parliament wanted to 'ban prayer rooms in public institutions of education' (Beslutningsforslag nr. B 54, 2017, and later B 152, 2017).

B 54 Forslag til folketingsbeslutning om forbud mod bederum på offentlige uddannelsesinstitutioner.[9]

7 https://lovkvalitet.dk/lovkvalitetsvejledningen/3-retlige-graenser-og-almindelige-principper/3-2-almindelige-retsprincipper/3-2-1-principper-der-bygger-paa-grundloven/3-2-1-1-singulaer-lovgivning, accessed 1 November 2019.

8 This section draws on Vinding, "Discrimination of Muslims in Denmark" in Saral & Bahçecik (eds.), *State, Religion and Muslims: Between Discrimination and Protection at the Legislative, Executive and Judicial Level* (Leiden: Brill, 2020).

9 "B54, Forslag til folketingsbeslutning om forbud mod bederum på offentlige uddannelsesinstitutioner," p. 1., https://www.ft.dk/ripdf/samling/20161/beslutningsforslag/b54/20161_b54_som_fremsat.pdf, accessed 1 November 2019.

Fremsat den 18. januar 2017 af Marie Krarup (DF), Alex Ahrendtsen (DF), Tilde Bork (DF), Jens Henrik Thulesen Dahl (DF), Kristian Thulesen Dahl (DF), Søren Espersen (DF), Marlene Harpsøe (DF), Christian Langballe (DF), Merete Dea Larsen (DF) og Peter Skaarup (DF).

Folketinget pålægger regeringen inden udgangen af indeværende folketingsår at fremsætte lovforslag om forbud mod bederum på alle offentlige uddannelsesinstitutioner.

Explicitly and regardless of any concern for discrimination against Muslims, the proposal states that "… the purpose of the proposal is that the parliament should ensure that no public education institution—from primary school to higher education—supports Islamic social control and thus further Islamisation of Danish society."

In its motivation for the proposal, the Danish People's Party yet again demonstrated its biased view and very limited understanding of Islam and Muslims, not to speak of the actual and reasonable situation regarding prayer rooms in Denmark.

> In the Muslim tradition, there is a strong tradition of checking whether others obey the holy law, the Sharia. In Denmark, we call it social control. Public educational institutions should not support social control by designing rooms that are used as prayer rooms. They will provide the opportunity to check whether a pupil or student is using these prayer rooms, and whether the exercise takes place according to special rituals.[10]

The reason for the proposal and the preceeding controversy was that a number of Muslim students had filed a discrimination complaint with the Board of Equal Treatment. Their school had issued a general ban on all religious functions and rituals during school hours, because the group of students had been praying in empty classrooms and in the main corridor of the school, which gave rise to conflict. In early February 2015, a group of seven or eight students had gathered to pray, which on various occasions had delayed teaching and disrupted a class in progress. Amongst those praying were people from outside the school, and there were concerns that the students would try to coerce or harass other Muslim students into joining the prayers. In early March 2015, the

10 "B54, Forslag til folketingsbeslutning om forbud mod bederum på offentlige uddannelsesinstitutioner," p. 2, https://www.ft.dk/ripdf/samling/20161/beslutningsforslag/b54/20161_b54_som_fremsat.pdf, accessed 1 November 2019.

school issued new guidelines on 'collective and personal conduct.' The school argued that these rules were non-discriminatory, but the result of a strategic effort, which aligned their rules with those of other educational institutions. The goal was to make the school a respectful, tolerant and inclusive space open to all. However, because these new rules banned political and religious activities, including 'mission and the demanding and controlling of a religious code of conduct,' and thus indirectly targeted Muslim prayer, the students filed a complaint with the Board of Equal Treatment in May 2015.[11]

While the Board of Equal Treatment did not uphold the students' complaint, there was a minority opinion. One member argued that the school had not justified the rules, had not demonstrated the gravity of the interruptions, had not sought alternative solutions and had not tried to mediate the conflict. Nonetheless, the majority of the Board held that the episodes did cause 'disturbance, conflict and insecurity,' and that out of concern for the cohesion and diversity of the students and after consulting the student body, the school was justified in issuing the new rules. In reporting the arguments in the case, the Board of Equal Treatment found judicial precedent in a Supreme Court ruling from 2001 (U2001.83H) upholding a school ban on collective prayer in common halls and areas.

11 Board of Equal Treatment, j.no., 2015-6811-24330, https://www.retsinformation.dk/Forms/R0710.aspx?id=192312, accessed 1 November 2019.

CHAPTER 7

Burial and Cemeteries

The Danish parliament legislates for the affairs of the Church of Denmark, and ecclesiastical law issues like burial and the use of buildings and cemeteries are part of public law. Much of such ecclesiastical legislation also explicitly regulates the affairs of other religious minorities. As regards rules and regulations for minorities, Muslims included, on burial and cemeteries, the main body of law is found in the *Act on Church of Denmark buildings and cemeteries* (LBK no. 1156, 1 September 2016), the *Act on burial and cremation* (LBK no. 43, 17 Jauary 2020), as well as related executive orders and circular letters regarding burial and cemeteries of the Church of Denmark. For example, the *Act on Church of Denmark buildings and cemeteries* (LBK no. 1156, 1 September 2016) specifies the general responsibilies regarding cemeteries. Section 9 specifies that the day-to-day authority to oversee and maintain cemeteries rests with the Parish Council, whereas the Minister of Ecclesiastical Affairs makes the rules regulating the construction, extension, decommissioning, fencing, organisation, planting and maintenance of cemeteries.

7.1 Cemeteries[1]

Generally, religious groups have the right to have a place assigned for burials and, according to Danish law, the Minister for Ecclesiastical Affairs may allocate such land. Since 1975, there has been space reserved for Muslim burials in 16 municipal or church cemeteries in Denmark which were originally consecrated as Christian (Jacobsen 2014, 200). Since 1996, religious communities outside the Church of Denmark have been granted the right to organise their own burial rituals and procedures by way of organised cemetery boards. Currently, the rules and regulations for setting up a religious burial ground are contained in the *Act on the Religious Communities outside the Church of Denmark* (LOV 1533, see also above):

1 This section draws on Jacobsen 2014 and on Vinding 2020, "Discrimination of Muslims in Denmark" in Saral & Bahçecik (eds.), *State, Religion and Muslims: Between Discrimination and Protection at the Legislative, Executive and Judicial Level* (Leiden: Brill, 2020).

§ 6. Et trossamfund kan efter ansøgning til kirkeministeren få tilladelse til at anlægge og drive egne begravelsespladser.
Stk. 2. En ansøgning i henhold til stk. 1 skal ledsages af en vedtægt om bestyrelse, tilsyn og benyttelse m.v. af begravelsespladsen, herunder oplysninger om de særlige forhold, der gør sig gældende i henseende til gravstedernes udformning og beståen. Vedtægten skal godkendes af kirkeministeren. En tilladelse til anlæg af begravelsesplads forudsætter endvidere, at det pågældende areal er erklæret egnet til anlæg af begravelsesplads af Styrelsen for Patientsikkerhed.
Stk. 3. Kirkeministerens tilladelse efter stk. 1 kan bl.a. betinges af, at der stilles sikkerhed for begravelsespladsens vedligeholdelse. Sikkerhedens art og størrelse fastsættes af kirkeministeren.
Stk. 4. Kirkeministeren fastsætter nærmere regler om oprettelse af begravelsespladser for trossamfund.

It was not until 2006 that the Danish Islamic Burial Foundation managed to set up an independently owned and operated Muslim cemetery outside Copenhagen (Jacobsen 2014, 200). The association has 6,000 members. At the site there is room for between 6,000 and 8,000 graves, and so far there are more than 400 graves. While about half of the 350 Muslims who die every year in Denmark are flown back to their countries of origin to be buried, the Danish Islamic Burial Foundation expects the number of deaths—and thus the number of Danish burials—to rise in the near future to about 2,000 a year (Jacobsen 2014, 200).

7.2 Other Religious Funerals and Burials

As demonstrated above, the *Act on the Religious Communities outside the Church of Denmark* clearly gives the Minister of Ecclesiastical Affairs the power to approve applications by religious communities to establish and run their own cemeteries. Yet, the general rules and regulations for funerals and burials still apply. The specifics of regulating religious funerals and burials are found in the *Act on burial and cremation* (LBK no. 43, 17 Jauary 2020) and the *Executive order on burial and cremation* (BEK no. 593, 1 December 1975), and the details are specified in the *Circular letter on burial and cremation* (CIR 220, 1 December 1975). These regulations apply to all, and cited and highlighted below are the sections and details that are specific to religious communities other than the Church of Denmark.

The *Act on burial and cremation* (LBK no. 43, 17 Jauary 2020) specifies that dead bodies must be buried or cremated (section 1) and that burial must take place in either the cemeteries of the Church of Denmark or other approved cemeteries (section 2). If the deceased is a member of the Church of Denmark or another religious community, it is automatically assumed that the body is to be buried during a religious ceremony, unless there is an explicit request for a civil funeral, that is, one without the presence of a priest or religious official of the community (section 8). If a priest or religious official of another religious community does participate and the burial takes place at one of the cemeteries or chapels of the Church of Denmark, then the funeral ceremony must be negotiated with the board of the cemetery (section 11). Section 15 states that the board of a Church of Denmark cemetery may, with the permission of the Minister of Ecclesiastical Affairs, designate a part of it for use by a religious community outside the Church.

Bekendtgørelse af lov om begravelse og ligbrænding (LBK nr 43 af 17/01/2020)[2]
§ 1. Lig skal enten begraves eller brændes.
§ 2. Begravelse skal ske på folkekirkens kirkegårde eller andre af kirkeministeren godkendte gravpladser.
Stk. 2. Gravsætning i kirker eller dertil hørende gravkapeller eller krypter kan dog ske, hvor dette hidtil har været særlig hjemlet eller under særlige omstændigheder tillades af kirkeministeren.

[…]
§ 7. Begravelsesmyndigheden afgør på grundlag af den fremsatte anmodning og under iagttagelse af reglerne i § 8, om begravelse eller ligbrænding skal finde sted, og om en præst skal medvirke ved begravelseshandlingen (kirkelig begravelse) eller denne skal foregå uden medvirken af en præst (borgerlig begravelse).
§ 8. Ved afgørelse af, om liget skal begraves eller brændes, skal ønsker, som afdøde har fremsat efter sit fyldte 15. år, efterkommes.
Stk. 2. Ved afgørelse af, om begravelseshandlingen skal være kirkelig eller borgerlig, skal ønsker, som afdøde har fremsat efter sit fyldte 15. år, efterkommes. Var afdøde ved sin død medlem af folkekirken eller et trossamfund uden for folkekirken, anses dette som udtryk for et ønske om kirkelig begravelse, medmindre det modsatte godtgøres.
Stk. 3. Foreligger der ingen tilkendegivelser fra afdøde med hensyn til de i stk. 1 og 2 nævnte spørgsmål, skal ønsker herom fra den, der fremsætter

2 https://www.retsinformation.dk/Forms/R0710.aspx?id=152547, accessed 1 November 2019.

anmodningen om foretagelse af begravelse eller ligbrænding, efterkommes, medmindre en person, der stod afdøde nærmere, fremsætter et herfra afvigende ønske.

[...]
§ 11. Ved kirkelig begravelse fastlægges begravelseshandlingens forløb af præsten efter forhandling med den, der ønsker begravelsen eller ligbrændingen foretaget.
Stk. 2. Når en præst i folkekirken medvirker, skal begravelseshandlingen dog foretages i overensstemmelse med folkekirkens jordpåkastelsesritual.
Stk. 3. Når en præst i et trossamfund uden for folkekirken medvirker ved en begravelse på folkekirkens kirkegårde eller fra dens kapeller, skal der ved fastlæggelsen af begravelseshandlingens forløb tillige forhandles med kirkegårdsbestyrelsen.

[...]
§ 15. Bestyrelsen for en folkekirkelig kirkegård kan med kirkeministerens tilladelse overlade en del af denne til brug for et trossamfund uden for folkekirken.
§ 16. Kirkeministeren kan tillade anlæg af kommunale begravelsespladser. På sådanne begravelsespladser skal der af kommunen opføres mindst ét begravelseskapel, medmindre der alene skal ske urnenedsættelse på begravelsespladsen. Folkekirkens præster og præster i trossamfund uden for folkekirken kan foretage begravelse på pladsen.
Stk. 2. Kirkeministeren kan under ganske særlige omstændigheder tillade anlæggelse af andre begravelsespladser end de i stk. 1 nævnte.
Stk. 3. Tilladelser efter stk. 2 kan bl.a. betinges af, at der stilles sikkerhed for begravelsespladsens vedligeholdelse. Sikkerhedens art og størrelse fastsættes af kirkeministeren.
Stk. 4. For de i stk. 1 og 2 nævnte begravelsespladser fastsættes regler om bestyrelse, tilsyn og benyttelse m.v. i en af kirkeministeren eller i særlige tilfælde på anden måde efter kirkeministerens nærmere bestemmelse.

In the *Executive order on burial and cremation* (BEK no. 593, 1 December 1975) some of the rules regarding burial and cremation are further specified. Article 6, subsection 2, is of great importance for the many Muslims who seek to be buried abroad, because the 'priest'—that is the word used in the legislation for a religious official of the community—may perform the religious ceremonies expediency. This helps to quicken the process and allows Muslims to conduct their rituals for the deceased.

Bekendtgørelse om begravelse og ligbrænding (BEK nr 593 af 01/12/1975)[3]

§ 4. Det skal fremgå af anmodningen, om liget skal jordfæstes eller brændes, og om en præst skal medvirke ved begravelseshandlingen (kirkelig begravelse) eller denne skal foregå uden medvirken af en præst (borgerlig begravelse). Anmodningen skal for så vidt angår de nævnte forhold være i overensstemmelse med ønsker, som afdøde har fremsat efter sit fyldte 15. år, jfr. herved stk. 2.
Stk. 2. Var afdøde ved sin død medlem af en ligbrændingsforening eller lignende sammenslutning, skal dette—medmindre andet godtgøres—anses som udtryk for ønske om ligbrænding. Ligeledes skal medlemskab af folkekirken eller et trossamfund uden for folkekirken—medmindre andet godtgøres—anses som udtryk for ønske om kirkelig begravelse.
[…]
§ 6, stk 2, […] Skal liget føres til en anden del af landet eller til udlandet, udleveres til anatomisk brug eller omstændighederne iøvrigt taler derfor, kan kirkelig begravelseshøjtidelighed dog finde sted forinden attestens udstedelse, såfremt den præst, der skal forrette begravelsen, efter de foreliggende oplysninger finder, at betingelserne for hans medvirken er til stede.

The full details of burial and cremation and many of the related issues are regulated in the *Circular letter on burial and cremation* (*To the bishops, county officials and the Copenhagen magistrate*) (CIR 220, 1 December 1975). These are of special interest when considering the practical detail regarding religious burials in religious communities outside the Church of Denmark.

Cirkulære om begravelse og ligbrænding. (Til biskopperne, amtmændene og Københavns magistrat) (CIR nr 220 af 01/12/1975)[4]

IV. Begravelseshandlingen.
[…]

2. Begravelseshandlingens forløb.
[…]

3 https://www.retsinformation.dk/Forms/R0710.aspx?id=72280, accessed 1 November 2019.
4 https://www.retsinformation.dk/Forms/R0710.aspx?id=72384, accessed 1 February 2020.

b. Kirkelig begravelse i trossamfund uden for folkekirken.
Bestemmelsen i lovens § 11, stk. 1, hvorefter begravelseshandlingens forløb fastlægges af præsten efter forhandling med den, der ønsker begravelsen eller ligbrændingen foretaget, gælder også ved begravelser inden for trossamfundene, og det er således også i disse tilfælde præsten som den for begravelseshandlingens forløb ansvarlige, der har den endelige afgørelse.
Den hidtidige ordning, hvorefter kun præster inden for anerkendte trossamfund og ikke-anerkendte kristne trossamfund kunne få adgang til at foretage begravelse på folkekirkens kirkegårde eller fra dens kapeller, er udvidet, således at nu præster for alle trossamfund uden for folkekirken har adgang til at foretage begravelser på folkekirkens kirkegårde eller fra dens kapeller, jfr. lovens § 11, stk. 3.
Foretages begravelsen på folkekirkens kirkegårde eller fra dens kirker og kapeller, stilles der ikke som hidtil krav om, at begravelseshandlingen skal foretages efter folkekirkens ritual eller et af kirkeministeriet godkendt ritual. Derimod skal præsten foruden med den eller dem, der ønsker begravelsen foretaget, forhandle med kirkegårdsbestyrelsen om begravelseshandlingens forløb, jfr. lovens § 11, stk. 3. På kommunale begravelsespladser har alle trossamfunds præster ret til at foretage begravelse efter deres trossamfunds ritual, jfr. lovens § 16, stk. 1.
Den foran omtalte bestemmelse i lovens § 13, hvorefter kirkegårdsbestyrelsen kan modsætte sig sådanne led i en påtænkt begravelseshandling, som ville stride imod den sømmelighed og orden, der bør iagttages på kirkegårde, gælder også med hensyn til begravelseshandlinger på trossamfundenes egne kirkegårde. Iøvrigt er det som hidtil overladt til de uden for folkekirken stående trossamfund selv at fastsætte nærmere bestemmelser om udførelse af begravelseshandlinger på deres egne kirkegårde.

This circular letter makes it clear that, as opposed to the earlier regulations of 1975, "priests from all religious communities outside the Church of Denmark have access to the cemeteries or chapels of the Church of Denmark," and it is no longer a requirement that the rituals of the Church of Denmark be followed. The only major limitation is that such burial acts or rituals outside the Church of Denmark must be in accordance with the decency and order associated with regular cemeteries.

For better or worse, it is very hard for religious communities to sort their affairs regarding burial without working closely with the officals and clergy of the Church of Denmark. While some may find it problematic that the Church of Denmark is involved, another common sentiment is that the officials and clergy, as well as undertakers and others, are very professional and very much appreciate the situation.

CHAPTER 8

Education and Schools

Article 76 of the Constitution guarantees freedom of education as "a right for all children to receive a free education." Most parents or guardians enroll their children in the public schools (*Folkeskolen*), but those who want to make their own educational arrangements for their children are free to do so. Education is mandatory for every child, but the freedom to choose schooling is a special right for parents to give their children the necessary instruction either at home or in a private school. Most who do not choose the public schools choose a private school for political, religious, cultural, pedagogical, national or personal reasons, as provided for in the *Act on Free Schools and Private Elementary Schools* (LBK 1111, 30 August 2018). However, there are core parts of the curriculum that must be followed and educational standards that must be met as part of the requirement for education.

8.1 Religion in Compulsory Education

The mandatory elements of education mean that all children in the country must receive an education, regardless of whether they attend public or private schools. The purpose, curriculum and teaching standards are defined in the *Act on the Public School* (folkeskoleloven).

> Bekendtgørelse af lov om folkeskolen (LBK nr 823 af 15/08/2019)[1]
>
> (Folkeskolens formål)
> § 1. Folkeskolen skal i samarbejde med forældrene give eleverne kundskaber og færdigheder, der: forbereder dem til videre uddannelse og giver dem lyst til at lære mere, gør dem fortrolige med dansk kultur og historie, giver dem forståelse for andre lande og kulturer, bidrager til deres forståelse for menneskets samspil med naturen og fremmer den enkelte elevs alsidige udvikling.
> Stk. 2. Folkeskolen skal udvikle arbejdsmetoder og skabe rammer for oplevelse, fordybelse og virkelyst, så eleverne udvikler erkendelse og fantasi og får tillid til egne muligheder og baggrund for at tage stilling og handle.

1 https://www.retsinformation.dk/Forms/R0710.aspx?id=209946, accessed 1 November 2019.

Stk. 3. Folkeskolen skal forberede eleverne til deltagelse, medansvar, rettigheder og pligter i et samfund med frihed og folkestyre. Skolens virke skal derfor være præget af åndsfrihed, ligeværd og demokrati.
[...]
§ 6. Kristendomsundervisningens centrale kundskabsområde er den danske folkekirkes evangelisk-lutherske kristendom. På de ældste klassetrin skal undervisningen tillige omfatte fremmede religioner og andre livsanskuelser.
Stk. 2. Et barn skal efter anmodning fritages for at deltage i undervisningen i kristendomskundskab, når forældremyndighedens indehaver skriftligt over for skolens leder erklærer selv at ville sørge for barnets religionsundervisning. Fritagelse kan normalt kun ske fra begyndelsen af et skoleår. Er barnet fyldt 15 år, kan fritagelse kun ske med barnets samtykke. Undervisningsministeren kan fastsætte regler om, hvilken procedure der skal følges ved fritagelse for kristendomskundskab.

As highlighted above, the purpose of public school is to give the students the abilities and skills to prepare them for further education and learning, to give them a deep understanding of Danish culture and an understanding of other countries and their cultures. Subsection 3 stresses that "the public school must prepare students for participation, co-responsibility, rights and duties in a society of freedom and democracy. Thus, the school's affairs must be characterised by intellectual freedom, equality and democracy." From time to time, in political debates, these words have been understood by some to mean in opposition to certain Islamist ideas.

The Act also defines the subject entitled 'Christian studies' and the core of this is the Christianity of the Evangelical-Lutheran Church of Denmark. In the later years of schooling, the subject also includes other religions and life stances. Subsection 2 spells out the right to withdraw children from Christian studies.

While Islam is not explicitly mentioned, the subject and content descriptions of what a teacher must know to be able to teach is detailed. Teachers who wish to be able to teach the subject in school must gain the required competences in 'Christian studies/religion' to BA level at a teacher training college. This is defined in the *Exective Order on the Education of Bachelors as Teachers in the Public Schools.*

Bekendtgørelse om uddannelsen til professionsbachelor som lærer i folkeskolen (BEK nr 1068 af 08/09/2015)[2]

2 https://www.retsinformation.dk/Forms/R0710.aspx?id=174218, accessed 1 February 2020.

Kristendomskundskab/religion
Kristendomskundskab/religion omhandler religionsdidaktik og forskellig brug af religion, filosofi og etik, historisk og aktuelt, anskuet i dansk, europæisk og globalt perspektiv og med menneskers kollektive og individuelle verdens- menneske- og samfundsopfattelser i både religiøse og ikke-religiøse sammenhænge og de handlinger, der er forbundet hermed.

Kompetenceområder
Kompetenceområde 1: Religionsdidaktik
Kompetenceområde 2: Undervisning i emnet kristendom
Kompetenceområde 3: Undervisning i emnet islam og andre religioner
Kompetenceområde 4: Undervisning i emnet filosofi, herunder etik og ikke-religiøse livsanskuelser

The subject is defined as including the teachings of religion, the different uses of religion, philosophy and ethics, historically and currently, as seen from Danish, European and global perspectives. Teachers who wish to teach Islam must specialise in competence area three on 'teaching in the subject of Islam and other religions.' The content of this is defined as "[t]eaching the subject of Islam and other religions concerns Islam and other religions in the present and past, local and global, religious innovation and as a teaching topic," which includes Islam as a world religion, Islam as a contemporary religion in Denmark and the central imagery, rituals, myths and culture of Islam.

8.2 Religious Education

During the eighth grade, the subject of 'Christian studies' is not taught, as the Church of Denmark offers a weekly preparation class for those students who seek confirmation. Traditionally this is a kind of catechetics and it is not mandatory, but does take up time in the class schedule. Muslim students and others who do not want to be confirmed in the Church will have the time off.

Mosques and other Islamic religious communities may offer religious education outside school at the same time, after school or during the weekends, but this is not regulated by law or administrative orders.

8.3 Private Schools

In Denmark, religious communities may offer teaching and schooling according to the education curriculum standards in private or free schools and do so on the basis of their religious ethos. They receive public subsidies if they fulfil prescribed conditions as to the teaching and curriculum, the quality of instruction, independence and executive administration. They cannot be controlled by special interests, must not abandon main of the curriculum and must promote democracy in education. Donations must be disclosed publicly, they are subject to inspection and control, and it is not allowed for such schools to cooperate with extraneous institutions or groups which are not relevant to the curriculum. As brought to attention through recent media coverage and political debate, there have been cases of this with some religious free schools, including Muslim ones, which have been closed down by the authorities, after Ministerial inspection has shown them to be failing the public standards.

Bekendtgørelse af lov om friskoler og private grundskoler m.v. (LBK nr 816 af 14/08/2019)[3]

§ 1. Friskoler og private grundskoler (frie grundskoler) kan inden for rammerne af denne lov og lovgivningen i øvrigt give undervisning, der stemmer med skolernes egen overbevisning, og tilrettelægge undervisningen i overensstemmelse med denne overbevisning. Skolerne afgør inden for de samme rammer frit, hvilke elever de vil have på skolerne.
Stk. 2. Frie grundskoler giver undervisning inden for børnehaveklasse og 1.–9. klassetrin, som står mål med, hvad der almindeligvis kræves i folkeskolen. Skolerne skal efter deres formål og i hele deres virke forberede eleverne til at leve i et samfund som det danske med frihed og folkestyre samt udvikle og styrke elevernes demokratiske dannelse og deres kendskab til og respekt for grundlæggende friheds- og menneskerettigheder, herunder ligestilling mellem kønnene. Skolerne kan tillige omfatte 1-årig undervisning på 10. klassetrin.

According to section 1 of the *Free Schools Act*, "free schools and private elementary schools (free elementary schools) can within the framework of this act and the law in general provide education that corresponds to the school's own convictions and organise teaching in accordance with this conviction." Free

3 https://www.retsinformation.dk/Forms/R0710.aspx?id=209870, accessed 1 November 2019.

schools may choose to use religious, political or pedagogical persuasion as the foundation or ethos for their school, which usually means greater diversity. If the schools adhere to the national standards and accept the supervision of the Ministry of Education, they qualify for public funding for such education. In Denmark, there are 550 free schools with about 110,000 pupils.

For Muslims in Denmark, as well as for other religious groups, this allows them to form their own schools according to their religious convictions. This freedom may be expressed directly as either a confessional statement in their charters, in their practice or indirectly through the ethnicity or religion of the students and parents of a particular school. As of October 2017, there were 29 free schools with an explicitly Muslim foundation or Islamic ethos.

In recent years, however, such Muslim free schools have attracted significant political attention. At the beginning of the publication of diverse media stories relating to the schools and their conduct, management or practice, critical politicians expressed great concern about the academic levels, the schools' world view, misconduct and the misappropriation of public funds or the lack of social cohesion or responsibility. The current political argument against such free schools is that such alleged malpractice is possible only because the schools may freely choose whom to hire and who may enrol. This allows them to choose—and effectively discriminate among—staff and students socially, academically and religiously. Following such argument—and disregarding the legal framework for significant autonomy for such schools—politicians, debaters and critics argue that religious free schools help to bring about parallel religious societies detrimental to the socialisation in the general Danish public schools. Through such arguments concerning differential intake and social control the critics can also explain away and dismiss the demonstrated successes and achievements of Muslim free schools.

Recent controversies concern the amendment to the Free Schools Act in 2016, whereby then Minister for Childen, Teaching and Equality, Ellen Trane Nørby, sought to improve the quality of the free elementary schools to make it clear in their statements of purpose that they must "strengthen the democratic education of the pupils" and "prepare pupils to live in a society like the Danish with freedom and government, and develop and strengthen students' knowledge of and respect for fundamental freedoms and human rights, including gender equality" (L36, 2016). This enacted amendment is yet another manifestation of the political agreements that came about in the spring of 2016, including the efforts to "curb those religious preachers, who seek to undermine Danish laws and values and support parallel legal beliefs." In addition, the amendment increases control over and inspections of free schools.

CHAPTER 9

Further and Higher (Tertiary) Education

There are no explicit statutes or administrative law on Islam in higher education, nor on any other religious communities for that matter, except for the theology programme related to the Church of Denmark. This seems to be part of the Danish model of equal treatment amongst other religious communities. The closest in terms of legal documents are the curriculum and study programmes for the MA in Islamic Studies at the University of Copenhagen, and the corresponding classes at other universities in Denmark.[1]

Quoted here is a section from the Faculty of Humanities' Curriculum for the Master's Programme in Islamic Studies, which defines the Master in Islamic Studies as a two-year full-time programme including a dissertation, totalling an expected 3,300 work hours. The purpose of the Master's Programme is to give thorough and research-based teaching in fields and subjects relating to Islamic theology, law, mysticism, history, sociology, politics and ideology with the emphasis on the 20th and 21st centuries. Graduates are expected to have a high level of professional skills and insights into Islam of relevance to a career in integration, journalism, research, teaching, public and private companies as well as national and international NGOs, working with Muslims and/or the Islamic world. This obviously includes aspiring Muslim leaders and graduates, who might be seeking chaplaincy positions.

Studieordning for kandidatuddannelsen i Islamiske Studier, 2008-ordningen[2]

§1. Normering
Kandidatuddannelsen i Islamiske Studier er et 2-årigt fuldtidsstudium normeret til 120 ECTS-point, hvoraf 90 ECTS-point udgøres af det centrale fag inkl. speciale, og 30 ECTS-point udgør kandidattilvalget.

---

1 Vinding 2016, *Islamforskning og islamiske studier på Københavns Universitet*, Tidsskrift for Islamforskning (TIFO), Årg. 10 Nr. 1 (2016): Dansk islamforskning anno 2016, 21–35. https://tifoislam.dk/article/download/24870/21777/, accessed 1 November 2019.

2 https://hum.ku.dk/uddannelser/aktuelle_studieordninger/islamiske-studier/islamiske_studier_ka.pdf, accessed 1 November 2019.

Stk. 2. ECTS-point (European Credit Transfer System-point) angiver den arbejdstid, som gennemførelsen af et uddannelsesforløb er normeret til. 60 ECTS-point svarer til 1 års heltidsstudier svarende til 1.650 arbejdstimer.

§ 9. Kompetenceprofil for den færdige kandidat
Kandidatuddannelsen i Islamiske Studier giver en grundig indføring i en række emner inden for islamisk teologi, jura, mystik, historie, sociologi, politik og ideologi med hovedvægten lagt på det 20. og 21. århundrede.
Kandidaterne stifter i deres studium indgående kendskab til islamisk teologi, jura, mystik, historie, sociologi, politik og ideologi i såvel muslimske majoritets- som minoritetssamfund med hovedvægt lagt på det 20. og 21. århundrede.
Målet med kandidatuddannelsen i Islamiske Studier er at uddanne humanistiske kandidater, der har en professionel og videnskabeligt baseret kompetence i islamiske forhold på et højt niveau og er rustede til at varetage professionsudøvelse inden for en række fagområder (integrationsområdet, journalistisk, forskning, undervisning, statslige og private virksomheder såvel som nationale og internationale ngo'er), der arbejder i den islamiske verden.

There are no legally established facilities or instruments for the training of teachers for Islamic religious education and there is no established Islamic religious education in Denmark. There are no private universities in Denmark.

There is private, religiously based training and education in Islam available through some of the mosques, some of the Islamic religious communities as well as through aspiring "Islam academies", but numbers are small and proper confessional higher education in Islam is sought internationally.

9.1 Imam Training in Public Tertiary Education

There has been much debate on imam training in Denmark, going back as far as the late 1990s. Continuing imam training is politically understood to be a de-radicalising tool, and the education is often vaguely imagined by analogy with the pastoral training offered to pastors from the Church of Denmark after finishing their theology degrees from the secular universities in Denmark.

Opinion makers from the religious communities, including Muslim ones, and professors from the Faculty of Theology at the University of Copenhagen proposed in 2015 a flexible Master's Programme with a selection of subjects and classes on Islamic theology and forms of practice, but based on individually composed curricula.[3] Currently, it is a structured but individually planned programme laid down according to the academic regulations of the Master's Programme at the Faculty of Theology, and is currently the closest there is to university imam education in Denmark.[4]

---

3 Politiken, 26 August 2015, https://politiken.dk/indland/art5586871/Universitet-%C3%A5bner-master-i-islamisk-teologi, accessed 1 November 2019.

4 "Masteruddannelse ved Det Teologiske Fakultet" https://teol.ku.dk/uddannelser/master_som_fleksibelt_forloeb/om_uddannelsen/Master_TEO_2009_retningslinjer_revideret_marts_2016_godkendt.pdf, accessed 1 February 2020.

CHAPTER 10

Islamic Chaplaincy in Public Institutions

Chaplaincy in public institutions in Denmark is almost solely an issue for the Evangelical-Lutheran Church of Denmark. This is both a historical and sociological fact. During the 19th and 20th centuries priests from the Church of Denmark sought to provide spiritual care for those who could not come to church services, but this was increasingly institutionalised and secularised through the second half of the 20th century. By way of extension from this Christian institution, Muslim chaplaincy began in 1997.[1]

In Danish, the term chaplain as such is not used. Rather, in parallel to the titles given to priests, Danes colloquially speak of "prison imam" or "hospital imam," or simply "religious preacher." The first Muslim chaplain in Denmark was a convert by the name of Leon Soudhari Hansen, who was employed by a Copenhagen prison first as a teacher and then from 2002 as imam. Much of the need for Islamic chaplaincy and indeed the first few imams employed were encouraged by the Lutheran chaplains, who had experienced issues and difficulty in helping Muslim patients or inmates.

10.1 Schools

There has been no public discussion about Islamic chaplains in Danish public schools as there are no other chaplains in schools. However, at the eight major universities in Denmark there are associated some 15 full-time or part-time priests of the Church of Denmark. Hitherto, there have been no Islamic chaplains associated with Danish universities.

10.2 Hospitals

With 57 major and minor hospitals across five regions, Denmark has more than 110 full-time or part-time Church of Denmark priests who serve the reli-

1 Reintoft Christensen, Kühle & Vinding, "Christianity and Islam in Danish Prisons—A Case of Secular Professionalisation of Chaplaincy," in Zwilling, A.-L., *Religion and Prisons in Europe*. EUREL publication (Berlin: Springer Verlag, 2020).

gious and spiritual needs of the more than 1.3 million admissions each year. By comparison, there is only one Muslim chaplain.[2] He is Naveed Baig and is employed at the *Rigshospitalet,* Denmark's largest hospital in Copenhagen, where he is also the coordinator of the Ethnic Resource Team, which consists of 40 volunteers from different ethnic and religious backgrounds. They are counsellors and interlocutors in relation to patients and relatives with similar backgrounds.

10.3 Prisons

The right to participate in religious services in prison is specified in section 35 of the *Enforcement of Sentences Act 2012*, and section 41 regulates the kinds of employment that inmates may be given with due regard to religious affiliation.

Straffuldbyrdelsesloven, LBK nr 1242 af 11/11/2015[3]

Deltagelse i gudstjenester m.v.
§ 35. En indsat har ret til at deltage i gudstjenester, der afholdes i institutionen. Såfremt ordens- eller sikkerhedsmæssige hensyn gør det påkrævet, kan kriminalforsorgsområdet dog nægte bestemte indsatte adgang til at deltage i gudstjenester og begrænse antallet af deltagere. Hvis det besluttes at begrænse antallet af deltagere, skal de pågældende indsatte så vidt muligt i stedet have adgang til at overvære gudstjenesten via elektroniske medier.
Stk. 2. En indsat har ret til samtale med en præst eller lignende fra sit trossamfund.
[...]

§ 41. Justitsministeren fastsætter regler om de indsattes beskæftigelse, herunder om, at beskæftigelsespligten skal tilrettelægges under hensyn til de indsattes religiøse tilhørsforhold.

2 https://www.dr.dk/mitliv/naveed-er-danmarks-eneste-hospitalsimam-jeg-gaar-haand-i-haand-med-doeden, accessed 1 November 2019.

3 https://www.retsinformation.dk/forms/r0710.aspx?id=170653, accessed 1 November 2019.

See also:

Bekendtgørelse om ophold i varetægt, BEK nr 1037 af 23/06/2016[4]

Deltagelse i gudstjeneste m.v.
§ 25. En varetægtsarrestant, som ikke er isoleret i medfør af retsplejeloven, har ret til at deltage i gudstjenester, der afholdes i institutionen. Såfremt ordens- eller sikkerhedsmæssige hensyn gør det påkrævet, kan kriminalforsorgsområdet dog nægte bestemte varetægtsarrestanter adgang til at deltage i gudstjenester og begrænse antallet af deltagere. Hvis det besluttes at begrænse antallet af deltagere, skal de pågældende varetægtsarrestanter så vidt muligt i stedet have adgang til at overvære gudstjenesten via elektroniske medier.
Stk. 2. En varetægtsarrestant har ret til samtale med en præst eller lignende fra sit trossamfund, medmindre politiet af hensyn til varetægtsfængslingens øjemed modsætter sig det.

Sections 35 and 41 respectively regulate religious services and employment for inmates, with concern for their religious needs. Section 35—and the corresponding article in the executive order on incarceration, article 25—grants the right to participate in religious services in accordance with international regulations on prison, such as the United Nations Rules for the Treatment of Prisoners and the European Prison Rules. Also, inmates have the right to speak with a priest or 'similar' from their own religious community. This is limited only by concern for order and safety and, alternatively, electronic media services and counselling may be provided. Section 41 delegates to the Minister of Justice the power to specify the rules for inmates' employment in prison.

Cirkulære om ansættelse af og tilsyn med religiøse forkyndere i Kriminalforsorgen (CIRIH nr 9106 af 02/03/2018)[5]

Kapitel 1
Dækningsområde mv.
§ 1. Dette cirkulære omfatter religiøse forkyndere, som tilhører andre trossamfund end den evangelisk-lutherske danske folkekirke (herefter religiøse forkyndere), der ansættes i kriminalforsorgsområderne.

4 https://www.retsinformation.dk/Forms/R0710.aspx?id=181983, accessed 1 November 2019.
5 https://www.retsinformation.dk/Forms/R0710.aspx?id=198405, accessed 1 November 2019.

§ 2. Tilkaldelse af religiøse forkyndere kan som hidtil ske ad hoc, jf. straffuldbyrdelseslovens § 35, stk. 2.
Stk. 2. Ad hoc-tilkaldelse af religiøse forkyndere sker som udgangspunkt ved hjælp af kriminalforsorgsområdets øvrige religiøse forkyndere og kan finde sted efter den indsattes anmodning om en konkret religiøs forkynder, i det omfang det er muligt.
§ 3. Hvis der ikke er en autoritativ myndighed inden for det pågældende trossamfund/religion, som kan varetage tilsynet på en måde, der modsvarer biskoppen i den evangelisk-lutherske danske folkekirke, gælder reglerne i dette cirkulære vedrørende ansættelsesprocedure, tilsyn mv.
[...]

Ansættelsesprocedure
§ 5. Ansættelse af religiøse forkyndere sker efter opslag og afholdelse af ansættelsessamtaler m.v.
§ 6. Ved udvælgelse og ansættelse af religiøse forkyndere nedsætter kriminalforsorgsområdet et lokalt ansættelsesudvalg. I ansættelsesudvalget kan Direktoratet for Kriminalforsorgen deltage med en repræsentant i det omfang, det skønnes nødvendigt for at sikre, at der er en ensartet praksis for ansættelse af religiøse forkyndere.
§ 7. Hvis der ikke er en autoritativ religiøs myndighed inden for det pågældende trossamfund/religion, kan en eller flere af direktoratet særligt udpegede sagkyndige personer desuden medvirke under ansættelsessamtalerne.
Stk. 2. De sagkyndige personer skal rådgive ansættelsesudvalget om ansøgerens indsigt i religiøse og kulturelle forhold og om den pågældende ansøgers evne til at varetage den religiøse betjening af indsatte, herunder afholdelse af religiøse handlinger, sjælesorgssamtaler og eventuel studiekreds på tjenestestedet.
§ 8. For at vurdere den enkelte ansøgers faglighed kan ansættelsesudvalget stille krav om, at ansøgeren giver en prøve på den relevante religiøse handling svarende til prøveprædiken for præster i folkekirken.
§ 9. Inden ansættelse skal religiøse forkyndere, ligesom andre medarbejdere i Kriminalforsorgen, trækkes i kriminalregisteret og underskrive en tavshedspligterklæring.
§ 10. Ansættelse foretages af kriminalforsorgsområdet.
Stk. 2. Kriminalforsorgsområdet skal i tillæg til ansættelsesbrevet udarbejde en detaljeret beskrivelse af, hvad stillingen indebærer for at sikre, at kriminalforsorgsområdet og den religiøse forkynder har en fælles forståelse af stillingens omfang og indhold. Stillingsbeskrivelsen skal

1) sikre, at den religiøse forkynder får nogle trygge rammer, indenfor hvilke stillingen kan varetages,
2) sikre, at ledelsen har overblik over den religiøse forkynders ansvarsområder, og
3) synliggøre den religiøse forkynders ansvarsområder overfor andre faggrupper, herunder synliggøre områder, hvor den religiøse forkynder på konstruktiv vis kan være andre faggrupper behjælpelig.
Stk. 3. Stillingsbeskrivelsen skal sendes i kopi til direktoratet.

Løn og ansættelsesvilkår
§ 11. Månedslønnede religiøse forkyndere med en udenlandsk uddannelse, som er på niveau med og er sammenlignelig med en uddannelse, der er omfattet af overenskomst for akademikere i staten, ansættes i henhold til overenskomst for akademikere i staten, hvis uddannelsen er en forudsætning for at bestride stillingen som religiøs forkynder.
[…]

Kapitel 4
Gejstligt tilsyn, sprog og opfølgning
§ 21. Religiøse forkyndere kan have en vigtig funktion som rollemodel for indsatte og kan derfor fungere som et vigtigt bindeled i forhold til indsattes integration i det danske samfund. Opgavevaretagelse i Kriminalforsorgens institutioner skal derfor altid foregå på en sådan måde, at opgavevaretagelsen bidrager til at fremme et demokratisk livssyn og forebygge ekstremisme og radikalisering hos de indsatte.
§ 22. Prædikener skal som udgangspunkt foregå på dansk. Faste bønner eller ordrette citater fra religiøse skrifter kan siges på et andet sprog end dansk.
Stk. 2. Udgangspunktet om, at prædikener skal foregå på dansk, kan fraviges i tilfælde, hvor størstedelen af de indsatte, der deltager i den religiøse handling, ikke forstår eller taler dansk. Tilladelse til at prædike på et andet sprog end dansk skal i det konkrete tilfælde gives af områdedirektøren, områdechefen for resocialisering eller chefen for den pågældende institution. Direktoratet skal underrettes om en given tilladelse snarest muligt. Gudstjenester for grønlandske indsatte kan i det hele afholdes på grønlandsk.
Stk. 3. Sjælesorgssamtaler med en religiøs forkynder kan foregå på et andet sprog end dansk.
[…]

Gejstlige tilsyn
§ 24. Religiøse forkyndere skal i lighed med folkekirkepræsterne underlægge sig et gejstligt tilsyn. Hvis der ikke inden for det pågældende trossamfund/religion findes en autoritativ myndighed, som kan varetage tilsynet på en måde, der modsvarer biskoppernes tilsyn med sognepræsterne, kan kriminalforsorgsområdet efter behov indkalde den enkelte religiøse forkynder til en samtale med repræsentanter fra kriminalforsorgsområdet, en medarbejder fra Direktoratet for Kriminalforsorgen og eksperter, som er kyndige inden for religion, radikalisering mv., med henblik på blandt andet at afdække den religiøse forkynders fortsatte egnethed til at varetage stillingen.

Dialogforum
§ 25. Kriminalforsorgsområdet skal som udgangspunkt sikre, at den religiøse forkynder deltager i et lokalt dialogforum på tjenestestedet med de øvrige religiøse forkyndere, herunder præster og ledelsen fra tjenestestedet og eventuelt generelt for religiøse forkyndere i Kriminalforsorgen. Deltagelsen i det lokale dialogforum medregnes i de religiøse forkynderes arbejdstid.

Kapitel 5
TV-transmission af religiøse handlinger
§ 26. Af hensyn til de indsatte, der af ordens- og sikkerhedsmæssige grunde ikke kan overvære religiøse handlinger, vil der så vidt muligt ske TV-transmission af religiøse handlinger fra en eller flere institutioner. Optagelserne vil blive udsendt til de indsatte, så de kan se de religiøse handlinger på cellens TV enten direkte eller som optagelse, der kan ses på et senere tidspunkt, hvis den indsatte ikke opholder sig i cellen på tidspunktet for den direkte udsendelse.
Stk. 2. De religiøse forkyndere, som ansættes i kriminalforgsområder, hvorfra udsendelserne transmitteres, skal i forbindelse med ansættelse forpligtes til at medvirke til TV-transmission.

Kapitel 6
Økonomi mv.
§ 27. Alle udgifter til aflønning af religiøse forkyndere—både ansatte og ad hoc tilkaldte—afholdes af kriminalforsorgsområdet.
§ 28. Kriminalforsorgsområdet skal så vidt muligt tilvejebringe lokalemæssige rammer for udøvelse af de indsattes religion. Udgifter hertil påhviler det enkelte område. Almindelig drift og vedligeholdelse af lokalerne, også af de løse genstande, påhviler ligeledes det enkelte område.

§ 29. Driftsudgifter til indkøb af religiøse skrifter og indretning af fællesrum til religiøse og kulturelle formål, herunder fx bederum og fodbad, afholdes endvidere af kriminalforsorgsområdet.

The circular letter on the 'Employment and oversight of religious preachers in the Prison and Probation services' of 2018 clearly sets out how to engage chaplains from other religious communities. Overall, the letter is concerned with establishing clear working conditions for the employment of chaplains in terms of rights, safe working environments, professional and collegial conditions and ongoing conversations with specialists and experts in the religious field, in lieu of what in the Church of Denmark would be a bishop with theological oversight. All of this is designed to enable the chaplain to perform his duties and responsibilities to the full. Of specific concern for Islam and Muslims and in light of the political developments in Denmark, with the increasing employment of Muslim chaplains in the Prison and Probation Services the circular letter deals with issues of prison security, proper training, radicalisation risks and extremism in prisons. Article 21 of the circular specifies that "religious preachers may serve an important function as role models for the inmates and may therefore work as an important connection in the integration of the inmates into Danish society. The job in the institutions of the Prison and Probation service must therefore always be handled in such a way that the performance of tasks contributes to the promotion of a democratic life stance and the prevention of extremism and radicalisation of inmates."

Closely corresponding to the circular letter on the employment and supervision of religious preachers, a similar circular letter of 2018 regulates a number of pracitical concerns and in great detail provides reasonable accommodation for access to worship, religious texts, dress, dietary requirements, holidays and more. In contrast to other, weightier legal documents, this circular letter clearly addresses specific Islamic aspects of prison life, such ritual washing before prayer, fasting from sunrise to sundown and temporary release from prison for Eid at the end of Ramadan.

Cirkulæreskrivelse om reglerne for indsattes adgang til udøvelse af religion i kriminalforsorgens institutioner (CIS nr 9105 af 02/03/2018)[6]
(Til kriminalforsorgsområderne)

6 https://www.retsinformation.dk/Forms/R0710.aspx?id=198359, accessed 1 November 2019.

Indledning
1. Nedenstående er en gennemgang af de regler, der gælder for gejstlig betjening af indsatte. Med gejstlig betjening forstås i denne sammenhæng egentlige religiøse aktiviteter som gudstjeneste/muslimsk fællesbøn og sjælesorgsamtaler/den personlige samtale og/eller deltagelse i en studiekreds.

Gejstlige handlinger, herunder bønner, rituel afvaskning og sprog
1.1 Indsatte har ret til at udøve deres religion i institutionerne.
Udøvelse af religion i form af eksempelvis bøn og rituel afvaskning samt anvendelse af religiøse rekvisitter skal som udgangspunkt foregå i den indsattes fritid, herunder i pauser i beskæftigelsestiden. Institutionerne skal dog udvise fleksibilitet, hvis der er indsatte, der ønsker at udøve deres religion i form af f.eks. bøn i arbejdstiden.
Personlige samtaler/sjælesorgssamtaler kan afholdes i indsattes beskæftigelsestid, såfremt den religiøse repræsentant ikke er til stede på tjenestestedet i indsattes fritid.
Prædikener skal som udgangspunkt foregå på dansk. Faste bønner eller ordrette citater fra religiøse skrifter kan siges på et andet sprog end dansk. Gudstjenester for grønlandske indsatte kan i det hele afholdes på grønlandsk.
Udgangspunktet om, at prædikener skal foregå på dansk, kan fraviges i tilfælde, hvor størstedelen af de indsatte, der deltager i den religiøse handling, ikke forstår eller taler dansk. Tilladelse til at prædike på et andet sprog end dansk skal i det konkrete tilfælde gives af områdedirektøren, områdechefen for resocialisering eller chefen for den pågældende institution. Direktoratet skal underrettes om en given tilladelse snarest muligt.
Sjælesorgssamtaler med en religiøs forkynder kan foregå på et andet sprog end dansk.

Nægtelse af deltagelse i gudstjenester m.v. eller begrænsning af antallet af deltagere
1.2 Såfremt ordens- eller sikkerhedsmæssige hensyn gør det påkrævet, kan kriminalforsorgsområdet nægte bestemte indsatte adgang til at deltage i gudstjenester og begrænse antallet af deltagere, jf. straffuldbyrdelseslovens § 35, stk. 1, 2. pkt.
Muligheden for begrænsning i antallet af deltagere er navnlig møntet på situationer, hvor det på grund af pladsmangel eller indsattes forskellige gruppetilhørsforhold ikke er forsvarligt at tillade alle de indsatte, som ønsker det, at deltage i gudstjenesten m.v.

Det forudsættes, at udvælgelsen af de indsatte, som nægtes adgang til en gudstjeneste m.v. på grund af pladsmangel eller gruppetilhørsforhold, sker ud fra objektive og saglige kriterier, herunder således at det så vidt muligt tilstræbes, at det ikke hver gang er de samme indsatte, der nægtes deltagelse.
[…]

Rum til religiøse formål, herunder til gudstjenester
1.3 Hvor det ikke er muligt at indrette et egentligt rum til religiøse formål, bør der så vidt muligt reserveres tider til udøvelse af gejstlige handlinger i et egnet rum. Der er ikke noget til hinder for, at et sådant rum deles af flere trossamfund. Rummet bør i så fald indrettes med henblik herpå, og inventaret og udsmykningen bør være egnet til afholdelse af religiøse handlinger, eventuelt med funktionelt flytbart inventar.

Religiøse skrifter
1.4 Kriminalforsorgsområdet skal sikre, at de indsatte har adgang til at låne et tilstrækkeligt antal religiøse skrifter.

Fritagelse for beskæftigelse
1.5 Alle indsatte, uanset religiøs observans, skal have mulighed for at være fritaget for beskæftigelse på deres religiøse helligdage.
I praksis kan det være vanskeligt at vurdere, hvilke dage det religiøse tilhørsforhold forbyder beskæftigelse, da der er mange forskellige fortolkninger og religiøse opfattelser inden for samme trosretning. Ligeledes er der mange religioner og trosretninger, som er mindre kendte. Dertil kommer, at der ikke nødvendigvis er en autoritativ person/myndighed, som kan give anvisninger på tvivlsspørgsmål. Den enkelte indsatte skal selv dokumentere/sandsynliggøre, at den dag, der ønskes fri, er en helligdag inden for pågældendes tro, hvorefter kriminalforsorgsområdet afgør sagen efter en konkret vurdering. Der henvises i øvrigt til Straffuldbyrdelseskontorets vejledning vedrørende religiøse helligdage.
Indsatte, hvis religiøse tilhørsforhold forbyder dem at være beskæftiget på visse dage, skal have tilrettelagt beskæftigelsestiden således, at de ikke beskæftiges på disse dage. Institutionen skal herefter så vidt muligt tilbyde de indsatte beskæftigelse på andre dage. Kriminalforsorgsområdet bestemmer, hvorledes de på anden måde skal opfylde arbejdstidsnormen, jf. § 5 i beskæftigelsesbekendtgørelsen.
[…]

Beklædning
1.6 Indsatte må ikke bære en beklædning, som gør det vanskeligt for personalet at identificere den indsatte og aflæse ansigtsudtryk m.v., hvis dette konkret skønnes uforeneligt med ordens- eller sikkerhedsmæssige hensyn, jf. genstandsbekendtgørelsens § 1, stk. 2. Personalet skal endvidere have mulighed for at se, hvordan den indsatte har det. Spørgsmålet om, hvorvidt der er ordens- eller sikkerhedsmæssig risiko forbundet med anvendelse af beklædningen, skal afgøres konkret, således at eksempelvis en beklædning, der dækker ansigtet, godt kan accepteres, hvis personalet i den konkrete situation ikke er i tvivl om, hvem den pågældende er, og der i øvrigt ikke skønnes at være ordens- eller sikkerhedsmæssig risiko forbundet med anvendelsen af beklædningen i den givne situation. Personale af samme køn som den indsatte kan i den forbindelse eventuelt bede den indsatte tage beklædningen af i et lokale, hvor der ikke er andre indsatte til stede, med henblik på at sikre sig, hvem den pågældende er.
Indsattes beklædning må i øvrigt ikke udgøre en sikkerhedsmæssig risiko ved udførelsen af arbejdsopgaver på kriminalforsorgens arbejdspladser.

Kost og drikke
1.7 Indsatte har ret til at indtage kost eller undlade at indtage kost, som er begrundet i kulturel eller religiøs tradition. Der henvises til § 5 i cirkulæret om forplejning af indsatte, som ikke er omfattet af selvforplejning i fængsler og arresthuse. Det fremgår heraf, at der ved tilberedningen og udleveringen af kosten så vidt muligt skal tages hensyn til indsattes særlige religiøse overbevisning.
I religiøse fasteperioder, hvor indsatte faster mellem solopgang og solnedgang, bør måltiderne så vidt muligt tilrettelægges således, at de indsatte, såfremt fasteperioden falder i sommermånederne, hvor det er længe lyst, kan få madpakker eller lignende, som kan indtages efter solnedgang og inden solopgang, og dermed på et tidspunkt, hvor der normalt ikke uddeles mad i institutionerne, jf. § 5, stk. 2, i ovennævnte cirkulære.
Under fasteperioder, hvor indsatte ikke indtager væske mellem solopgang og solnedgang, bør stikprøvevis urinprøvekontrol af indsatte så vidt muligt foretages inden solopgang eller efter solnedgang.

Udgang
1.8 Indsatte i åbne fængsler bør regelmæssigt have mulighed for deltagelse i gudstjeneste uden for institutionen, hvis der ikke afholdes gudstjeneste i institutionen, jf. udgangsbekendtgørelsens § 78, stk. 3.

Der kan lejlighedsvis gives indsatte, der i lukket institution har tilladelse til uledsaget udgang, kortvarig udgang med henblik på at overvære gudstjenester uden for institutionen, jf. udgangsbekendtgørelsens § 79. Kompetencen til at tillade udgang til gejstlige handlinger følger af de almindelige regler i udgangsbekendtgørelsens kapitel 2.
Indsatte, der tilhører andre trossamfund end den evangelisk-lutherske danske folkekirke, og som opfylder betingelserne for regelmæssig weekendudgang, kan få en udgang forlænget en gang om året med sammenlagt højst to dage i forbindelse med en religiøs højtid af en vis tyngde, fx afslutningen af Ramadanen.

10.4 Confidentiality

For all chaplains, both Christian and Muslim, the question of qualified confidentiality is important. Priests or imams are obliged to speak with inmates, in accordance with section 35, subsection 2, above, but have other chaplaincy responsibilities as well. To that end, they enjoy specially qualified and absolute confidentiality as defined in the 2014 *Procedural Code*.

Retsplejeloven, (LOV nr 737 af 25/06/2014)[7]
[...]

§ 170. Mod dens ønske, som har krav på hemmeligholdelse, må vidneforklaring ikke afkræves præster i folkekirken eller andre trossamfund, læger, forsvarere, retsmæglere og advokater om det, som er kommet til deres kundskab ved udøvelsen af deres virksomhed.
Stk. 2. Retten kan pålægge læger, retsmæglere og advokater, bortset fra forsvarere i straffesager, at afgive vidneforklaring, når forklaringen anses for at være af afgørende betydning for sagens udfald, og sagens beskaffenhed og dens betydning for vedkommende part eller samfundet findes at berettige til, at forklaring afkræves. Sådant pålæg kan i borgerlige sager ikke udstrækkes til, hvad en advokat har erfaret i en retssag, som har været betroet ham til udførelse, eller hvori hans råd har været søgt.

7 https://www.retsinformation.dk/forms/r0710.aspx?id=163838, accessed 1 November 2019.

This specially qualified and absolute confidentiality may be violated by a court only in cases of national security, substantial danger to life, or the like. Historically, this provision has been applied to recognised or approved religious communities in Denmark, which means that unrecognised communities may not necessarily enjoy this qualified confidentiality.

CHAPTER 11

Employment and Social Law

While many of the principles of law and policy on Islam and Muslims in Denmark are expressed elsewhere in legal documents as shown above, the practical challenges of integration of immigrants, legal aliens, refugees as well as Islamic norms and ethics are found in employment and social law. The overall ambition of social and economic integration policy has focused on employment and it has become the one key responsibility of social workers to make sure that levels of education and employment are secured. Therefore, also, many of the conflicts and challenges of integration materialise in employment and are of relevance to Islam and Muslims in Denmark. We see this in law and case law on discrimination, equal treatment, reasonable accommodation and social integration policy.

11.1 Non-discrimination

The legal area of rights and freedoms regarding religion in relation to the state naturally includes provisions for non-discrimination, and is arguably the most important aspect of the legal regulations between the state and Islam, especially as far as employment and the labour market are concerned. Freedom from discrimination is protected by Articles 70 and 71 of the Constitution, which prohibit discrimination on the grounds of race and religion, and specified in the executive order on the law prohibiting differential treatment on the labour market. It is part of the Danish effort to ophold and adhere to the international obligations on human rights and freedoms.

Bekendtgørelse af lov om forbud mod forskelsbehandling på arbejdsmarkedet m.v.[1]
(LBK nr 1001 af 24/08/2017)

Kapitel 1
Lovens anvendelsesområde
§ 1. Ved forskelsbehandling forstås i denne lov enhver direkte eller indirekte forskelsbehandling på grund af race, hudfarve, religion eller tro,

1 https://www.retsinformation.dk/eli/lta/2017/1001, accessed 1 November 2019.

politisk anskuelse, seksuel orientering, alder, handicap eller national, social eller etnisk oprindelse.
Stk. 2. Der foreligger direkte forskelsbehandling, når en person på grund af race, hudfarve, religion eller tro, politisk anskuelse, seksuel orientering, alder, handicap eller national, social eller etnisk oprindelse behandles ringere end en anden bliver, er blevet eller ville blive behandlet i en tilsvarende situation.
Stk. 3. Der foreligger indirekte forskelsbehandling, når en bestemmelse, et kriterium eller en praksis, der tilsyneladende er neutral, vil stille personer af en bestemt race, hudfarve, religion eller tro, politisk anskuelse, seksuel orientering eller national, social eller etnisk oprindelse eller med en bestemt alder eller med handicap ringere end andre personer, medmindre den pågældende bestemmelse, betingelse eller praksis er objektivt begrundet i et sagligt formål og midlerne til at opfylde det er hensigtsmæssige og nødvendige, jf. dog § 2 a.
Stk. 4. Chikane skal betragtes som forskelsbehandling, når en uønsket optræden i relation til en persons race, hudfarve, religion eller tro, politiske anskuelse, seksuelle orientering, alder, handicap eller nationale, sociale eller etniske oprindelse finder sted med det formål eller den virkning at krænke en persons værdighed og skabe et truende, fjendtligt, nedværdigende, ydmygende eller ubehageligt klima for den pågældende.

Section 1 clearly specifies the areas of application of the discrimination laws and what is understood by discrimination: "[f]or the purposes of this Act, discrimination means any direct or indirect discrimination based on race, colour, religion or belief, political opinion, sexual orientation, age, disability or national, social or ethnic origin." It explicitly mentions religion or belief, and goes on in subsections 2 and 3 to distinguish between direct and indirect discrimination. Direct discrimination is understood as "being treated worse than someone else is, has been or would be treated in a similar situation," and indirect discrimination is when "a provision, criterion or practice, which appears to be neutral, would render some persons inferior to others," and this is illegal unless "the provision, condition or practice in question is objectively justified by an objective purpose and the means for fulfilling it are appropriate and necessary."

The question of direct discrimination is relatively straightforward, and by means of this Act and the *Act on Ethnic Equal Treatment* 2009, a number of discrimination cases have been tried by the Board of Equal Treatment. Between 2010 and 2017 the Board of Equal Treatment heard 28 cases involving Islam and

Muslims.[2] However, the problematic cases concern indirect discrimination, which is much harder to prove, as indeed it is difficult to prove what appears neutral but is not. Also, arguments for objective justification must be heard, and the legal procedures are more complicated. Added to this, it is well established that there are financial and structural barriers to bringing cases about race, skin colour, religion or belief, or national or ethnic origin before the courts.[3]

Notwithstanding, a Muslim woman won a case on indirect discrimination that between 2010 and 2015 went right through the system from the Board of Equal Treatment all the way to the High Courts (U.2015.2984). They found that it was a violation of the *Discrimination Act* that the Muslim woman in training as a nutritionist could not be exempted from tasting pork.

The Muslim woman, who was born in Lebanon but grew up in Denmark, wore a scarf and in 2010 was training as a nutritional assistant at a vocational school. She did not want to taste the pork, but she was happy to prepare and cook it. With reference to a decision of its professional committee, the school required her to taste food with pork in it, although she did not have to eat the food, but was allowed to spit it out after tasting. When she refused on religious grounds, the school expelled her and the case came before the Equal Treatment Board. The woman argued that she had been subjected to discrimination on the basis of religion. The Equal Treatment Board found that the complaint was covered by the Discrimination Act, since the school ran a business in the form of vocational training. The requirement that the woman, like all other students, should taste the food, including pork dishes, made her, a Muslim, inferior to other pupils in terms of the chance of obtaining a nutritionist's education. She was awarded compensation. The school took the case to the City Court, which in 2013 found that since the woman did not want to taste pork for religious reasons, the requirement was indirect discrimination. In 2015, the High Court upheld the judgment on the same grounds as the City Court.

This is indeed a rare case. Both the Acts against discrimination and the jurisdiction of the Board of Equal Treatment apply mainly—if not solely—to the labour market. This has received significant international criticism. The *Sixth Periodic report on Denmark under the International Covenant on Civil and Political Rights* by the UN's Human Rights Committee (10 November 2015) recommended that Denmark improve the accessibility of effective remedies for any

2 As dicussed in Vinding, "Discrimination of Muslims in Denmark" in Saral, M. and Bahçecik, S.O. (eds), *State, Religion and Muslims. Between Discrimination and Protection at the Legislative, Executive and Judicial Levels* (Leiden: Brill, 2020).

3 "Domme og nævnssager om diskrimination på grund af etnicitet og handicap 2009–2014", Als Research APS September 2015, p. 47.

kind of discrimination, including expanding the mandate of the Board of Equal Treatment to all forms of discrimination.[4] In a similar vein, the European Commission against Racism and Intolerance in its *ECRI Report on Denmark* argued that "racist hate speech, in particular against Muslims, continues to be a problem," and highlighted that "under-reporting of hate speech is a problem that requires urgent attention."[5]

A sociological observation is relevant at this point. The concept which describes the Danish situation adequately is the notion of banal discrimination as introduced by Jim Beckford. He understands such discrimination as the routine, low-level, unthinking, but sometimes institutional discrimination that serves as a reminder and marker of the normal and is taken for granted.[6] Such discrimination keeps marginalising and alienating Muslims on a daily basis. The pure banality of such discrimination makes it almost impossible to address through the police or the authorities. The indirect and institutional nature of the banality makes it a handy political tool of what we might call effective politically organised discrimination. In a Danish legal context, such as the one that frames the legislative programme from 2016 onwards, it is impossible to distinguish between discrimination and the political discursive and even societal move towards a delegitimisation of Muslims in the public sphere.

Freedoms and rights are notoriously difficult to balance. Arguably, the main competence of a skilled jurist is to argue the balance between the rights of the one party against the violations of equal rights by another party. A case in point is the executive order that allows for the law on equal treatment of men and women on grounds of employment to be deviated from with respect to religious positions.

Bekendtgørelse om fravigelse af lov om ligebehandling af mænd og kvinder med hensyn til beskæftigelse m.v. for så vidt angår præstestillinger[7]
(*BEK nr 350 af 10/07/1978*)

4 Sixth Periodic report on Denmark under the International Covenant on Civil and Political Rights from UN's Human Rights Committee (10 November 2015), CCPR/C/DNK/CO/6, pp. 3, 7.

5 ECRI Report on Denmark, 16 May 2017, p. 9.

6 Jim Beckford, "Banal discrimination: Equality of respect for beliefs and worldviews in the UK," in D. Davis & G. Besier (eds.), *International perspectives on freedom and equality of religious belief* (Waco, TX: Dawson Institute of Church-State Studies, 2002).

7 "L38, Forslag til lov om ændring af lov om almene boliger m.v., lov om leje af almene boliger og lov om leje." https://www.retsinformation.dk/Forms/R0710.aspx?id=11550, accessed 1 November 2019.

> I medfør af § 11, stk. 1, i lov nr. 161 af 12. april 1978 om ligebehandling af mænd og kvinder m.v. fastsættes:
> § 1. Præstestillinger i folkekirken og dertil svarende stillinger inden for trossamfund undtages fra lovens område.

In straightforward language, the executive order allows for dispensation from the provisions of equal treatment between men and women when it comes to positions as priest in the Church of Denmark, but equally for corresponding positions in other religious communities. This echoes the European Court of Human Rights' jurisprudence, and much of the exemption from non-discrimination given in many domestic employment laws to the hiring of priests, but it is not uncontroversial.[8] For much conservative Muslim leadership this is a welcome exemption in a country where both secularism and anti-Islamic sentiments are common.

11.2 The Ghetto Plan

Commonly called the Ghetto plan, a Bill[9] was proposed by the government in 2018, as the then government's toughest social regulation to combat parallel communities and the assumed 'adverse impact of some Muslims'' practices of worship. Targeting at-risk public residential areas, the government proposed to employ a number of new initiatives for the development or dispersal of the 'hard ghetto areas.' The proposal also introduces tools for changing the mix of residents and housing in the at-risk residential areas. These include that the provision and rental rules are tightened and that recipients of certain public support are not allowed to move into these toughest ghetto areas. Finally, the proposal extends the rules governing the sale and demolition of properties that include public housing. The Bill is yet another initiative originating in the 2016 political agreement. The Bill was passed into law in November 2018.

The Bill's legal substance is quite diffuse, and in effect overlaps with other legislation proposed and enacted in 2017 and 2018, including the Act banning so-called re-education travel (see below), but the highlights were widely

8 Stuart, Alison, "Freedom of Religion and Gender Equality: Inclusive or Exclusive?" in *Human Rights Law Review*, 10 (2010), 429–459.

9 "L38, Forslag til lov om ændring af lov om almene boliger m.v., lov om leje af almene boliger og lov om leje." https://www.retsinformation.dk/Forms/R0710.aspx?id=11550, accessed 1 November 2019.

reported, thanks to the Government's own publication, 'One Denmark without parallel societies,' (*Ét Danmark uden parallelsamfund*).[10] Here, the government proposes to earmark funds for renovation, demolition and infrastructure changes needed to make extraordinary efforts in the vulnerable residential areas with a first priority for the ghetto areas. Funding must also be earmarked for the renovation of homes planned to be sold. Further, for the toughest ghetto areas there should be a target that the proportion of publicly subsidised housing be reduced to a maximum of 40 per cent by 2030. In order to enforce this, the state may order the housing association to initiate the liquidation of housing in the particularly stressed ghetto areas where, despite years of effort, it has failed to reverse negative developments in social problems, negative social control, crime, lack of education and employment.

In particular regarding security and crime, the government wants more police on the streets in the most problematic residential areas and is proposing a strategic effort to help to identify people who are particularly central to crime and security-creating behaviour in those areas. This is specified by means of a scheme that would allow the police to identify specific crime and insecurity areas where the punishment for certain forms of crime will be significantly increased for a period. Finally, they want to refuse criminals to take up residence in an exposed area and it should be possible more quickly and efficiently to evict tenants and members of a household other of whose members commit crime in and around the residential area in which they live.

While not mentioning Islam or Muslims at all, the report speaks at length about the cost of non-Western immigration, social control, increased social seclusion and lack of participation in public and social life. Much of this is hotly debated and contested, but it is ultimately a matter of social and integration policy. The report identifies 76,400 people as belonging to a 'parallel society.' As Jacobsen and Vinding argue in the chapter on Denmark in the *Yearbook on Muslims in Europe* 2019, however, the Government's indicators do not link these families' social status to any attitude to Danish society. No correlation is identified, and this considerably weakens credibility. The report established a number of socio-economic indicators that show different forms of inequality and social vulnerability. There is no research that shows that this social position coincides with the prevailing norms, thought or religion of society.[11]

---

10 https://www.regeringen.dk/media/4937/publikation_%C3%A9t-danmark-uden-parallelsamfund.pdf.

11 Jacobsen & Vinding 2019, pp. 205–207.

Nevertheless, then Minister of Immigration and Integration, Inger Støjbjerg, was not afraid to make the political motivation for this bill clear, demonstrating that it was built on the widely held political fiction that Sharia was encroaching on regular society, seeking to established parallel societies or jurisdictions. Her remarks on Muslims' practice of religion are a matter of opinion, but baseless and not supported by anything other than highly suspect insinuations and allusions that have been thriving in an anti-Muslim segment of Danish politics for quite some years. During the parliamentary debates on the Bill, she argued:

> Honestly, I think we might as well be straightforward and say that there are problems in parallel societies that originate from, and that also relate to, the way some Muslims have chosen to practise their religion. I don't think we should hide that, and I see that as a very, very big problem ... Of course, it is a problem, and it is a parallel society, resoundingly so. We should not stand for it.[12]

11.3 Social Inclusion Efforts by the Police Authorities

While the above-discussed 'ghetto plan' is indeed an expression of the Danish government's policies, the contrast to the social inclusion efforts being made by the police is remarkable. While still in legal effect, this circular letter on co-operation between the police and local Muslim communities continues to govern the policy of the police in this regard.

Samarbejde mellem politiet og muslimske lokalmiljøer (CIS nr 10234 af 24/10/2007)[13]

1. Indledning
Et tæt samarbejde mellem politi og lokalsamfund kan være en væsentlig faktor, når det gælder det danske samfunds indsats med henblik på at modvirke terrorangreb her i landet.
I den rapport om det danske samfunds indsats og beredskab mod terror, som blev afgivet i oktober 2005 af den tværministerielle arbejdsgruppe om terrorbekæmpelse, fremgår således som anbefaling 48 følgende:

12 https://jyllands-posten.dk/politik/ECE10429164/inger-stoejberg-mener-at-islam-skaber-parallelsamfund/, accessed 1 November 2019.
13 https://www.retsinformation.dk/Forms/R0710.aspx?id=113531, accessed 1 February 2020.

"Arbejdsgruppen anbefaler, at samarbejdet mellem det lokale politi og de muslimske samfund styrkes. Samarbejdet bør suppleres af skolefolk og socialarbejdere—bl.a. inden for rammerne af det eksisterende SSP-samarbejde."

Om baggrunden for anbefalingen anfører arbejdsgruppen bl.a., at det lokale samarbejde mellem politiet og de muslimske lokalmiljøer er væsentligt for en vellykket indsats mod radikalisering, og at det herigennem er muligt at opfange unge, der er i risiko for at udvikle en ekstremistisk eller destruktiv adfærd.

Det fremgår af regeringens handlingsplan for terrorbekæmpelse fra november 2005, at regeringen—med henvisning til arbejdsgruppens anbefaling—har til hensigt at styrke samarbejdet mellem det lokale politi og de muslimske lokalmiljøer, og at det nærmere vil ske ved, at Justitsministeriet ved en cirkulæreskrivelse til politiet foranlediger, at politikredsene søger at indlede et nærmere samarbejde med de muslimske samfund.

2. *Et styrket samarbejde mellem politiet og muslimske lokalmiljøer*

2.1. Justitsministeriet har i lyset af det under 1 anførte drøftet med Rigspolitiet, Politiets Efterretningstjeneste, og Det Kriminalpræventive Råd, hvordan samarbejdet mellem politiet og de muslimske lokalmiljøer kan styrkes.

[...]

Endvidere er der blevet peget på, at politiet i endnu større omfang end i dag bør have fokus på kulturforståelse—herunder at den muslimske befolkningsgruppe er mangfoldig og ikke en homogen gruppe—da kulturforståelse er af betydning bl.a. for det tillidsskabende politiarbejde i nærmiljøerne og kan være med til at nedbryde eventuelle fordomme. Kulturforståelse kan således ikke blot indgå i undervisningen på politiets grunduddannelse og i forbindelse med videreuddannelse, men kan også være et tema i de enkelte politikredse, hvor der f.eks. kan afholdes kurser og foredrag med kompetencepersoner fra de relevante lokalmiljøer, antropologer, arabister, turkologer eller lignende.

2.2. Iværksættelse af initiativer med henblik på et øget samarbejde med de muslimske lokalmiljøer, herunder også ved inddragelse af andre relevante myndigheder, bør have en klar ledelsesmæssig forankring, således at bl.a. medarbejderne i politiet og hos andre involverede myndigheder og ikke mindst de befolkningsgrupper, som initiativerne tager sigte på, oplever, at initiativerne har opbakning fra den øverste ledelse. Det vil f.eks. være

naturligt at drøfte initiativerne i de kreds- og lokalråd, der er oprettet som led i politireformen.
2.3. Justitsministeriet skal på den baggrund anmode politikredsene om—under nærmere hensyntagen til de lokale forhold—at søge at indlede et øget samarbejde med de muslimske lokalmiljøer.

Idekatalog til samarbejde mellem politiet og muslimske lokalmiljøer
1. Politiindsatsen
Politiindsatsen kan bruges konstruktivt i forhold til de muslimske lokalmiljøer.

Almindeligt politiarbejde
Politiet kan ved sin adfærd styrke relationer i lokalmiljøet og skabe tillid ved i ord og handling at vise, at politiet også er den muslimske del af befolkningens politi. Eksempelvis er det i forbindelse med kriminalitet rettet mod den enkelte borger vigtigt, at muslimske ofre for kriminalitet oplever, at de får den samme behandling og service fra politiet som andre ofre for kriminalitet.

Fokus på rollemodeller
Politiet kan i sit arbejde have fokus på de positive rollemodeller. Politiet kan f.eks. understøtte disse rollemodeller ved at gå i dialog med dem om deres mulige rolle som forbillede for andre og ved at introducere dem til foreningslivet, som er et centralt element i den danske kultur, og som kan være et godt udgangspunkt for integration mv.

Deltagelse i arrangementer i muslimske miljøer
For at undgå at politiet kun opleves i konkrete kriminalitetsrelaterede sammenhænge, kan politiet deltage i arrangementer i muslimske lokalmiljøer. Det kan være offentlige, kulturelle arrangementer, dialogmøder i moskéer, lørdagsskoler for muslimske kvinder mv.

Netværksstrukturer og dialogfora i lokalmiljøet
Politiet kan medvirke til at etablere konkrete netværksstrukturer og dialogfora i lokalmiljøet med det formål at drøfte problemstillinger i området. Afsættet herfor kan være henvendelser fra politiet til lokale foreninger og grupperinger, som f.eks. beboerforeninger, kulturelle foreninger, organiserede trossamfund og fædregrupper. Sådanne initiativer vil samtidig kunne understøttes af løbende elektronisk kommunikation som f.eks. oplysende e-mails fra politiet om relevante forhold og problemstillinger i lokalmiljøet.

"Mød dem, hvor de er"

Det er en grundlæggende problemstilling i forhold til initiativer mod terror, som er knyttet til lokalmiljøet, at de personer, der er involveret i ekstremisme eller er i fare for at blive involveret heri, typisk ikke er engagerede i lokalmiljøet og f.eks. ikke fast går i moské.

De pågældende kan i stedet opsøges på gadehjørner, på caféer og lignende steder, hvor de rent faktisk opholder sig. Politiet kan i det daglige arbejde være opmærksom på de områder, hvor marginaliserede eller utilpassede grupper almindeligvis opholder sig, og på de aktiviteter, som foregår på disse steder. I den forbindelse kan det være en god idé at skabe kontakt til medarbejdere de pågældende steder som f.eks. opsøgende socialarbejdere og fædregrupper, som kan være med til at forebygge, at de unge påbegynder en radikaliseringsproces.

Brug af "ungdomsgrupper"

Hvis der i lokalpolitiet er etableret en "ungdomsgruppe", som har særlig fokus på ungdomskriminalitet, kan denne gruppe spille en central rolle i opbygningen af netværk og tillid til unge med anden etnisk baggrund end dansk. I den forbindelse er tilstedeværelse, synlighed og dialog med de unge centrale nøgleord. Politiet vil f.eks. kunne være initiativtagere til aktiviteter for de unge for at afdramatisere relationerne mellem politiet og de unge og anskueliggøre faren ved radikalisering. Sådanne aktiviteter kan også være med til at give de unge alternative veje til at få kanaliseret eventuel vrede, som kan lede til radikalisering, over i noget positivt.

Kontinuitet

For at kunne etablere tillidsrelationer og gensidig respekt mellem politiet og de unge er det vigtigt, at der er en vis kontinuitet blandt de polititjenestemænd, som har med de unge at gøre. I forbindelse med konkrete problemstillinger i miljøerne, hvor politiet spiller den traditionelle rolle som retshåndhævende myndighed, vil det således være hensigtsmæssigt, at der så vidt muligt er en politimand/kvinde til stede, som har sin daglige gang i området og derfor allerede har en vis kontakt til miljøet.

2. Samarbejde med andre myndigheder, lokalforeninger mv.

SSP-samarbejdet

SSP-samarbejdet er et centralt redskab til at sikre en koordineret indsats mellem skole, socialforvaltning og politi. Gennem SSP-samarbejdet kan politiet medvirke til at sætte radikalisering på dagsordenen bl.a. med fokus på "tidlig bekymring" og dermed en hurtig SSP-indsats i forhold til eventuelle radikaliseringsprocesser. Det kan i den forbindelse drøftes, hvad radikalisering er, hvordan det kommer til udtryk, og hvordan de pågældende aktører kan forholde sig til det i praksis, herunder hvordan en tidlig koordineret indsats kan tilrettelægges mest hensigtsmæssigt. Som led i SSP-samarbejdet kan ekstremisme sættes på dagsordenen f.eks. i forbindelse med politiets besøg på skolerne, hvor ekstremisme kan indgå i tilknytning til oplæg og drøftelser om tolerance, racisme, religion mv.

Inddragelse af det øvrige lokalsamfund

Inddragelse af det øvrige lokalsamfund kan bidrage til en øget integration og dermed forebygge radikalisering. Det kan ske—eksempelvis i SSP-regi—i form af samarbejde med indvandrerforeninger, boligforeninger, sportsforeninger, ungdomsklubber eller borgerforeninger samt ved afholdelse af temamøder og gennemførelse af kampagner.

3. Etablering af partnerskaber i miljøerne

Partnerskaber med repræsentanter for muslimske lokalmiljøer

Der kan etableres partnerskaber med repræsentanter for de muslimske lokalmiljøer eventuelt suppleret med ad hoc ansættelse af ressourcepersoner, som kan indgå i samarbejdet mellem myndigheder og de muslimske lokalmiljøer om en tidlig indsats mod radikalisering. Ressourcepersonerne kan eksempelvis være klubmedarbejdere, integrationskonsulenter, muslimske skoleledere eller imamer.

Partnerskaberne kan medvirke til, at de muslimske miljøer føler ejerskab til og engagerer sig konkret i den forebyggende indsats mod terror. Partnerskaberne kan også bidrage til en erkendelse af, at der er tale om et fælles problem og derfor et fælles mål for politiet og lokalmiljøerne.

Brug af religion og personer med særlig indsigt heri i afradikaliseringsøjemed

Det har flere steder i udlandet vist sig relevant og virkningsfuldt at gøre brug af religion og personer med særlig indsigt heri i afradikaliseringsøjemed. Personer med særlig indsigt i religion kan i kraft af deres viden om islam med konkret afsæt i den religiøse tekst modargumentere og synliggøre alternative strategier. Dette giver mulighed for at konfrontere personer, der er på vej ud i en radikaliseringsproces, inden for samme terminologiske ramme, som den pågældende selv benytter, og dermed på den pågældendes egne præmisser. Politiet kan i samarbejde med repræsentanter for de muslimske lokalmiljøer pege på personer i lokalmiljøerne, som vil kunne udfylde en sådan rolle. Det bør i den forbindelse holdes for øje, at de pågældende ikke nødvendigvis er talerør eller repræsentanter for et givent muslimsk lokalmiljø. Erfaringerne viser, at særligt ungdommen generelt ikke føler sig repræsenteret af de lokale religiøse autoriteter.

The circular letter begins by confirming the findings of the cross-ministerial report of 2005 on Danish anti-terror efforts, which concludes with its recommendation that "the cooperation between the local police and the Muslim community should be strengthened" and that "cooperation should be complemented by school officials and social workers." To substantiate this, the circular letter highlights the importance of cultural understanding and including the Muslim population as a diverse, non-homogeneous group, which means that cultural understanding is crucial for the confidence-building police work in the local areas and may help to break down any prejudice, for the ultimate benefit of both police business and social cohesion and a sense of safety.

After emphasising that these principled and overall sentiments guide the whole of the effort, the letter promotes a 'catalogue of ideas' that may in very concrete and best-practice terms help to foster police co-operation with the Muslm community. It points to professionalism, courtesy and trust as the hallmarks of regular police business, but also to role models, active participation in Muslims' events and festivals, building networks and fora for dialogue and youth groups, 'meeting them where they are' and strengthening continuity, as well as working with other local groups and authorities.

It is far beyond the scope of these annotated documents to assess the effect and benefit of such initiatives, and some might say that this kind of thing does not work, but many who participate have little doubt that this indeed works. One thing is clear, however, namely that the remarkable dissonance between the top-down symbolic legislation and the bottom-up community work is counterproductive.

CHAPTER 12

Islamic Slaughter and Food Regulation

The question of halal food is particularly pertinent to Denmark, mainly because the meat industry and export is a very important business sector in traditionally rural Denmark. As part of the export business for poultry, the industry has substantially incorporated the practice of Islamic religious slaughter and halal certification, and it continues to be one of the significant political conflicts between Muslim practice and areas of Danish right-wing politics. Religious slaughter is permitted by articles 9, 10 and 11 in the executive order on slaughter and killing of animals. A number of regulations apply and the permit to perform religious slaughter is clearly defined. Despite this, *Time Magazine* wrote in 2015 that Denmark now bans religious slaughter.[1]

Bekendtgørelse om slagtning og aflivning af dyr (BEK nr 135 af 14/02/2014)[2]

Kapitel 1
Anvendelsesområde og definitioner
§1. Reglerne i denne bekendtgørelse finder anvendelse på slagtning og aflivning af dyr, der avles eller holdes med henblik på fremstilling af fødevarer, uld, skind, pelsværk og andre produkter.
[…]
Stk. 3. Ved slagtning efter religiøse ritualer forstås i denne bekendtgørelse slagtning hvor der anvendes en metode, som ikke er omfattet af forordningens bilag 1.

Kapitel 2
Generelle bestemmelser
§3. Dyr skal skånes for enhver undgåelig smerte, psykisk belastning eller lidelse under aflivning og dermed forbundne aktiviteter, jf. forordningens artikel 3, stk. 1.
[…]

1 *Time*, "Denmark Bans Kosher and Halal Animal Slaughter," 28 July 2015, http://time.com/3974498/denmark-ban-kosher-halal/, accessed 1 July 2019.
2 https://www.retsinformation.dk/eli/lta/2014/135, accessed 1 November 2019.

Kapitel 3

Slagtning og aflivning uden for slagterier

§ 6. Slagtning eller aflivning af dyr af hesteslægten, kvæg og strudsefugle må kun foretages af dyrlæger, slagtere, personer med jagttegn eller andre personer, der har modtaget uddannelse i slagtning eller aflivning.

Kapitel 4

Slagtning efter religiøse ritualer

§ 9. Kun dyr som omfattet af §§ 10 og 11, må slagtes efter religiøse ritualer. Slagtningen skal foregå med forudgående bedøvelse efter reglerne i denne bekendtgørelse. Det er endvidere en betingelse, at slagtningen foregår på et slagteri, og at kød eller andre dele fra et dyr helt eller delvist forventes afsat til eller afsat med henblik på videresalg til befolkningsgrupper, der efterspørger dyr slagtet efter religiøse ritualer.
Stk. 2. Dokumentation for afsætning eller forventet afsætning, jf. stk. 1, skal på forlangende kunne forevises for kontrolmyndigheden.

§ 10. Til bedøvelse af kvæg, får og geder kan slagteriet, inden dyret aflives endeligt ved afblødning, anvende en ikke-penetrerende boltanordning på følgende betingelser:
1) Den ikke-penetrerende boltanordning må ikke anvendes til dyr, der er under 8 måneder gamle eller til tyre, der er 24 måneder gamle eller derover.
2) Bedøvelsen skal udføres med et korrekt tryk og på et fastholdt dyr med fikseret hoved. Til fastholdelse af kvæg skal der anvendes en boks, hvor dyret fastholdes i opretstående stilling, således, at hoved og krop fikseres så skånsomt som muligt. Boksen og hovedfikseringen skal kunne justeres efter dyrets størrelse.
3) Såfremt bedøvelsen ikke forekommer efter første skud med en ikke-penetrerende boltanordning, skal dyret straks skydes med en penetrerende boltanordning eller bedøves ved brug af elektrisk strøm.
4) Afblødningen skal foregå ved, at begge halspulsårer og halsvener manuelt eller mekanisk overskæres med et skarpt redskab, umiddelbart efter, at dyret er bedøvet således, at dyret dør ved afblødning uden, at dyret på ny kommer til bevidsthed.

§ 11. Ved aflivning af slagtekyllinger med forudgående bedøvelse i vandbad skal slagteriet opfylde følgende krav i forbindelse med aflivningen:
1) Der må maksimalt gå et tidsrum på 5 sekunder fra at det enkelte dyr forlader vandbadet til at dyret rammer knivene.

2) Der skal sikres størst mulig ensartethed af slagtekyllingernes størrelse indenfor et slagtehold med det formål at øge bedøvelsens effektivitet.
3) Bedøvelsens effektivitet skal sikres, efter en på forhånd fastlagt procedure, ved opstart af hvert slagtehold og under afblødningen efter behov flere steder på slagtekæden. Af slagteriets standardprocedurer eller retningslinjer for god praksis skal tillige fremgå hvilke indikatorer, der skal indgå i vurderingen af bedøvelsens effektivitet.
4) Der skal sikres en øget ledningsevne i vandbadet ved hjælp af tilsætning af en saltopløsning eller anden opløsning med samme effekt ved opstart af en slagtekæde.
5) Der skal være mulighed for, at medarbejderne på en slagtekæde til stadighed kan kommunikere indbyrdes under aflivningsprocessen, herunder at der er sikret mulighed for hurtig standsning af slagtekæden ved behov, samt at der er sikret umiddelbar adgang til reserveudstyr til aflivning.
6) Indstillingen af de automatiske knive skal kontrolleres ved opstart af hvert slagtehold og løbende efter behov. Der skal ske systematisk vedligeholdelse af de automatiske knive, herunder efter behov udskiftning af knive. Stikningens effektivitet overvåges på baggrund af antal kyllinger, der ikke stikkes af den automatiske kniv.
7) Ved bedøvelse af slagtekyllinger i vandbad skal følgende elektriske parametre overholdes: Ved brug af pulserende jævnstrøm må frekvensen ikke overstige 600 Hz, og uanset strømtypen skal den gennemsnitlige strømstyrke pr. slagtekylling være mindst 100 mA. Dyrene skal udsættes for den pågældende strømstyrke i mindst fire sekunder. Både strømstyrke og frekvens skal som minimum kontrolleres ved opstart af slagtekæden og ved ændringer i størrelsen af dyrene på slagtekæden.
Stk. 2. De ovenfor under stk. 1, nr. 1–7, nævnte krav skal fremgå af slagteriets standardprocedurer eller retningslinjer for god praksis.
Stk. 3. Kravene i forordningen, bilag I, punkt 6.1 og punkt 6.2, finder uændret anvendelse.
Stk. 4. Fødevarestyrelsen kan i særlige tilfælde dispensere fra kravet i § 11, stk. 1, nr. 1, hvis helt særlige omstændigheder taler derfor.

The fact of the matter is that religious slaughter is permitted only if the animals in question—cattle, sheep or goats—have first been stunned by a non-penetrating stun gun, and that laughter by bleeding is executed swiftly and precisely so the animal never regains consciousness (as per article 10, above). For poultry the same principle applies. However, the stunning is done by submerging the animal in water which has a strong electric current running through it (as per article 11, above).

The question of weighing concerns about animal cruelty against the freedom of religion allowing religious slaughter is discussed both in the legal literature and in public. Zahle and Lund Hansen in their study of the different constitutional, human rights and animal rights concerns concluded that a statutory prohibition on ritual slaughter would be a limitation of the exercise of religious freedom. However, a prohibition on ritual slaughter which is justified by the desire to limit animals' anxiety and pain is justified by a consideration which may be in accordance with the requirements to limit religious practice.[3] Thus mechanical and electric stunning was introduced, which addressed most of the significant concerns for animal rights and ethics, and so there is no reasonable argument for limiting freedom of religion.

---

3 Zahle & Lund Hansen, "Rituel slagtning og religionsfrihed," in *EU-ret & Menneskeret 1998*, https://www.djoef-forlag.dk/publications/eumenneskeret/html/artikler/Art1998_2_058.htm, accessed 1 November 2019.

CHAPTER 13

Islamic Dress

Three issues regarding Islamic dress have found their way into Danish legal documents. The first concerns the limitations on religious headwear, such as headscarves, and has primarily been an issue for the labour market and a question for the courts. The second has to do with the appearance and impartiality of judges in court, which was regulated in the procedural code in 2009. The third concerns face-covering, such as the niqab and burka, which has been debated for some years, but was banned in 2018.

13.1 Scarves and Religious Headwear

The courts have ruled on a handful of questions regarding the headscarf, and three cases in particular seem to regulate the question. These are the Magasin case in 2000, the Toms case in 2001 and the Føtex case in 2005.

In 1998, a Muslim girl started her internship at the Magasin department store. However, when she turned up she was immediately dismissed on the ground that her headscarf was a violation of the department store's requirements for staff attire. This did not mean that staff had to wear a special uniform, but it was expected that the employees would be businesslike and nicely dressed, and that their attire would be in harmony with the supply of goods in the department. In the dress code it was specified that employees should not wear headwear. However, the court ruled in 2000 that in dismissing the Muslim girl for wearing a headscarf the Magasin department store was guilty of indirect discrimination.[1]

The second case concerned a Muslim girl who on religious grounds wore a headscarf and robes that covered everything but her hands and face. She had applied for a job at the chocolate and candy manufacturer Toms Fabrikker A/S but was unsuccessful. During an information meeting held regarding internships, she was informed that she would not be able to participate in the internship programme if she wore a scarf while working. Subsequently, an email to the plaintiff stated that it was not permissible to wear anything other than the

1 *Berlingske*, "Magasin tabte tørklæde-sag," 25 February 2003, https://www.berlingske.dk/samfund/magasin-tabte-toerklaede-sag, accessed 1 November 2019.

net cap which was used in production. This was part of the manufacturer's clothing and hygiene regulations. After some attempt by the Muslim girl to meet the requirements while still wearing her headscarf and robe, she left the training course and did not join the internship programme. She complained of indirect discrimination and argued that the dress code was not objective or proportionately required by the task she was doing and she made her suggestions for meeting the hygiene issues. The majority of the High Court found that the manufacturer was not in violation of the Discrimination Act because it had the right to define a dress code.[2]

After these two cases, the general impression was that prohibitions against headscarves were discriminatory unless proportionately rooted in hygiene or production requirements.[3] However, in the third case, the Føtex case, the Supreme Court found that a prohibition against headscarves was not in violation of the Discrimination Act. An employee of Moroccan origin started wearing a headscarf after several years of employment and was informed by the employer that this was in violation of her terms of employment. These included regulations that no headwear could be worn, and these had been enforced consistently.

The Supreme Court ruled that there was no unlawful indirect discrimination, as the dress code, which was consistently enforced against all employees, was "objectively justified for a fair purpose and the means to fulfill the purpose are appropriate and necessary." The Supreme Court stated, however, that formally neutral clothing rules particularly affect the proportion of Muslim women who wear headscarves for religious reasons. A 2017 ruling from the European Court of Human Rights (*Dakir v. Belgium* and *Belcacemi and Oussar v. Belgium*) ruled in favour of maintaining a full face-veil ban.

13.2 Judges in Courts

One special case in this regard is the so-called 'headscarves law' of 2009, which amended the Procedural Code to require judges to appear neutral and stop them from expressing religious or political affiliation while in court.

The law is based on a longer political discussion about judges in burka, which derives from an addition to the section on decorum requirements and expectation of personal appearance in the staff administrative guidance of the Danish Court Administration.

2 Eastern High Court ruling, 5 April 2001.

3 http://www.sjlaw.dk/nyheder/2005-nyheder/toerklaedeforbud-ikke-i-strid-med-lov-om-forbud-mod-forskelsbehandling/, accessed 1 November 2019.

The precise wording was decided by the Board of the Court of Justice at a meeting on 18 December 2007: "[a]s a common guideline, there is nothing to prevent employees of the Danish courts from wearing scarves, turbans or similar headgear for religious or cultural reasons as long as the face is not covered."[4]

This change was the specific reason for the Danish People's Party posting an advertisement under the heading, "This is known as justice," with a picture of a female judge wearing a niqab to show the Danes what in their view the consequences could be when judges were allowed to wear scarves.

In the autumn of 2008, the debate continued and on 19 December 2008 the Conservative Minister of Justice, Brian Mikkelsen, put forward his proposal to amend the Procedural Code,[5] inserting into it a new Article 56 which reads, "A judge must not appear at hearings in a manner that is apt to be perceived as an indication of the person's possible religious or political affiliation or of the person's attitude to religious or political matters in general."

> Lov om ændring af retsplejeloven (Dommeres fremtræden i retsmøder)
> I retsplejeloven, jf. lovbekendtgørelse nr. 1069 af 6. november 2008, foretages følgende ændring:
> Efter § 55 indsættes:
> »§ 56. En dommer må i retsmøder ikke fremtræde på en måde, der er egnet til at blive opfattet som en tilkendegivelse om den pågældendes eventuelle religiøse eller politiske tilhørsforhold eller om den pågældendes holdning til religiøse eller politiske spørgsmål i øvrigt.
> *Stk. 2.* Stk. 1 finder tilsvarende anvendelse på fuldmægtige, midlertidigt beskikkede dommere og de personer, der er nævnt i § 19, stk. 3.
> § 56 a. En dommer bærer kappe under hovedforhandlinger og retsmøder, der afholdes med henblik på sagens behandling i medfør af § 831.
> *Stk. 2.* Stk. 1 finder tilsvarende anvendelse på fuldmægtige og midlertidigt beskikkede dommere.«

In the government's comments on the Bill one can read about the purpose, validity and impact of the proposed law on the applicable law. Here it is stated that the purpose of the Bill is that judges appear neutral in order to "... support the general respect and confidence of the people in the courts".[6] The Bill was given its very specific wording and formulation, not because one does not trust

4 https://www.ft.dk/samling/20081/lovforslag/l98/20081_l98_som_fremsat.htm, accessed 1 November 2019.

5 Ibid.

6 Ibid.

judges to be independent and impartial, but because they must also appear to be so. The government does not believe that it is possible to wear religious symbols and, based on the discourses after the Muhammad cartoons crisis outlined above, arguing that in recent years religious issues have played an increasing role in the public debate in this country, among other things. in the light of the immigration of persons of different religious backgrounds, and that questions of religious affiliation, etc. in this context have generally become significantly more controversial than before.[7]

In the debates and hearings relating to the change to the Procedural Code in 2008 a number of concerns were raised, which may be summarised as follows.

First, respondents to the hearing statement generally do not believe that there is any reason to legislate and the comments also indicate that the area is already regulated in the courts' self-government rules, but this was not sufficient. The consultation parties from the trades unions in their response portray the change in law as an assault on the separation of powers, despite the fact that it was initially the parliament that had made the rules on administration of justice, which several parliamentary politicians also discuss in the further process of the Bill.

Secondly, the Procedural Code already contains rules on conflicts of interest, competence and reservations, so that the judge's complete impartiality must not be suspected.

Thirdly, the consultation responses note that the law is woefully inconsistent with its own purpose, for the ban does not apply to lay judges, because it is more important that they should as far as possible reflect a representative sample of the population. This is also already noted in the introductory remarks.

Fourthly, in the hearing, many, in particular the Council of Ethnic Minorities and the Danish Muslim Union, pointed out that the Bill discriminates against and makes different Muslim women who alone seem to wear religious attire.

Fifthly, the already very narrow scope of the Bill is further restricted when it is clear in the preliminary remarks that:

> Bestemmelsen omfatter ikke enhver fremtræden, som det er muligt at fortolke som en meningstilkendegivelse om religiøse eller politiske anliggender eller som et (ubevidst) udslag af dommernes personlige holdning til sådanne spørgsmål. Bestemmelsen omfatter alene adfærd og påklædning m.v., som er *egnet* til at blive *opfattet* af andre som en *tilkendegi-*

7 Ibid.

> *velse* om dommerens eventuelle religiøse eller politiske tilhørsforhold [...] Opfattelsen hos de tilstedeværende under det pågældende retsmøde eller dommerens egen bevæggrund er således ikke i sig selv afgørende for en vurdering af, om den pågældende adfærd eller påklædning er omfattet af forbuddet, idet der skal være tale om synlig påklædning, udsagn eller adfærd i øvrigt, som alment opfattes som motiveret af at ville vise et bestemt religiøst tilhørsforhold m.v. [...][8]

The applicability of the law is thus limited by three factors, all of which must be present and all of which must depend on discretion in specific cases, if the law is one day to be applied. Behaviour and attire must (1) be of a nature as (2) to be widely perceived by others as (3) motivated by wanting to show a particular religious affiliation. The essence of the law is that judges in hearings—motivated by showing their religious affiliation—must not appear in such a way as possibly to make others believe that they are religious, not because the judge must not be religious, but because others might think that a judge who looks religious would not judge fairly and according to the applicable law. Nor is it that the judge is not allowed to draw attention to his religion in general, for the Bill applies only to hearings. The validity of the law does not extend to the many other situations in which a judge may act. Nor is there anything inherent in religion that should cause one to think about the judge as impartial, as both the remarks and the hearing partners point out. The Bill identifies only the general perception of judges' particular and presumably premeditated behaviour as illegal.

On the whole, it must be said that the material content—that is, what the law actually prohibits—borders on the non-existent beyond those particular cases of female Muslim lawyers, who would want to seek judgeships and keep wearing their headscarves. It is almost pure formality, and the absurd cases that could be considered justifiable would already fall foul of the decorum requirement and expectation of personal appearance in the Courts' administrative guidance for their personnel. Furthermore, the Bill must be regarded as almost impossible to enforce in a court of law because the validity and applicability of the law rest on a threefold estimate of presumed factors in a situation, which itself is unlikely.

8 "Bemærkninger til lovforslaget," italics in original. https://www.ft.dk/samling/20081/lovforslag/l98/20081_l98_som_fremsat.htm, accessed 1 November 2019.

13.3 The Ban on Face Covering

On 31 May 2018 a majority in the Danish Parliament adopted a ban on face covering, which in effect is and has been discussed as a ban on wearing the niqab or burka. The ban, which amends the Danish Criminal Code, comes after renewed discussions which took place in 2017 and 2018. The question of criminalising the wearing of a burka or niqab was discussed in 2009 and 2010, but the debate quietened down after an academic report had concluded that a maximum of 200 women wore a burka or a niqab in Denmark.[9] The applicability of the section has been significantly limited and does not apply where a qualifying purpose is found. Nevertheless, during the first year, a total of 23 fines were issued.[10]

> Forslag til Lov om ændring af straffeloven (Tildækningsforbud)[11]
>
> §1 I straffeloven, jf. lovbekendtgørelse nr. 977 af 9. august 2017, som ændret senest ved lov nr. 141 af 28. februar 2018, foretages følgende ændringer:
> 1. I *§134 b, stk. 3,* ændres »der foretages for at beskytte mod vejrliget, eller som tjener andet anerkendelsesværdigt formål« til: »der tjener et anerkendelsesværdigt formål.«
> 2. Efter §134 b indsættes: »§134 c. Den, som på offentligt sted bærer en beklædningsgenstand, der skjuler vedkommendes ansigt, straffes med bøde.
> *Stk.* 2. Det i stk. 1 nævnte forbud gælder ikke for tildækning af ansigtet, der tjener et anerkendelsesværdigt formål.«

In the preparatory remarks, the Ministry of Justice discussed how freedom of speech and freedom of religion and belief came into consideration. "To the extent that covering the face in itself is regarded as an expression of opinion, it may be protected by freedom of speech. This should be included in the assessment of whether the cover serves a qualifying purpose. Similarly, it will be

9 "Rapport om brugen af niqab og burka," 2009, https://hum.ku.dk/faknyt/nyheder_fra_2010/2010/brugen-af-niqab-og-burka.pdf, accessed 1 February 2020.

10 *Ekstra Bladet*, "Burkaforbud fylder år: Så mange bøder er der givet," 31 July 2019, https://ekstrabladet.dk/112/burkaforbud-fylder-aar-saa-mange-boeder-er-der-givet/7731836, accessed 1 November 2019.

11 http://www.justitsministeriet.dk/sites/default/files/media/Pressemeddelelser/pdf/2018/lovforslag_tildaekningsforbud.pdf, accessed 1 February 2020.

included in the assessment of whether covering the face takes place in a way—and in a concrete context—closely related to the exercise of religious freedom, etc. It is assumed that covering the face for religious reasons as a clear starting point is not prohibited when it comes to a specific religious act or the like, for example, in a religious building or in connection with a wedding or funeral ritual, etc. Outside such concrete religious contexts—including, for example, normal transport to and from the place of a religious act—it will not suffice to refer to the fact that the face is being covered for religious reasons."[12] In this commentary by the Ministry of Justice, it is quite clear that the circumstances in which the ban applies are limited, and there is considerable room for interpretation by the individual police officer. The commentary and subsequent instructions to police officers[13] about qualifying purposes include fancy dress parties, freedom of speech and freedom of religion, especially as regards worship. In addition, it is left up to the individual officer to assess whether this is a criminal matter at all or a matter for social services:

> If the police suspect that the person is subject to negative social control, for example, in connection with a breach of the ban on cover, i.e., because the person expresses compulsion or other pressure to wear face-covering clothing, then the police must assess whether there is a basis for investigating a criminal offence or whether the person should be offered help and support, and so on.[14]

All in all, this Bill and amendment are designed—in part—to provoke and discourage the 'Islamist elements' and—in part—to satisfy right-wing politicians and voters. Both are obviously symbolic uses.

The law on banning face-covering came into force on 1 August 2018. In 2017, the three-party centre-right minority government, its ally, the Danish People's Party, and the main opposition party, the Social Democrats, voted for a ban on face covering. This effectively meant a ban on the niqab and burqa. On the day the law came into force, more than 1,000 people rallied to decry what they saw as an erosion of civil liberties, while a small demonstration of around five people celebrated what they felt was a long overdue measure.

---

12 Cited, p. 17, author's translation, http://www.justitsministeriet.dk/sites/default/files/media/Pressemeddelelser/pdf/2018/lovforslag_tildaekningsforbud.pdf, accessed 1 February 2020.

13 "Vejledning om Politiets håndhævelse af tildækningsforbuddet," https://politi.dk/tildaekningsforbud, accessed 1 February 2020.

14 Ibid.

Much of this legislation has been criticised vociferously by leading representatives from the Church of Denmark, minority religious groups, civil and human advocates and much of the legal profession. The legislative agenda in these and related areas of law targets Muslims and Islam in Denmark, if not directly then indirectly. In sum, it is lasting evidence of the anti-immigrant and anti-Muslim sentiments that influenced the former Liberal-Conservative government and continue to be part of the governing politics in Denmark.

CHAPTER 14

Criminal Law

In Danish criminal law we find another clear expression of anti-Muslim sentiment, following the May 2016 Agreement Paper. This includes criminalising explicit approval of certain punishable actions as part of religious education. However, an additional number of issues potentially or presumably relevant for Islam and Muslims are addressed in the criminal code, including travel for 're-education,' forced marriage and other instances of illegal coercion.

14.1 Criminalising Explicit Approval

As part of the May 2016 Agreement Paper, the government and the Social Democrats, the Danish People's Party and the Conservative People's Party proposed initiatives aimed at religious preachers who seek to undermine Danish laws and values and support parallel judgments. They argue:[1]

> The agreement means that in the future it must be punishable explicitly to support terror, killings, rape, acts of violence, incest, paedophilia, false imprisonment, coercion and polygamy as part of religious education. This applies regardless of whether the statements are made in private or in public. The agreement also means that both the activities of religious preachers and those of others acting as part of religious education must be covered by the criminalisation.

Therefore, a particular scenario was explicitly made criminal by way of a Bill amending the Criminal Code. The political ambition of the Agreement Paper found its legal form in the regulation making it illegal to 'expressly approve certain criminal acts as part of religious education,' with an added list of such criminal acts, by reference to Articles in the Criminal Code. The wording is peculiar as incitement to hatred or to violence, for example, is already a criminal offence, whereas, on the other hand, much of the Danish political establishment has been championing freedom of speech as an absolute right. This amendment falls right between these two positions, yet the most significant

1 Agreement Paper, op. cit., p. 5.

criticism concerns the fact that it merely regulates the religious aspects of condoning criminal acts, and not political or other public condoning of criminal acts.

> L18, Forslag til Lov om ændring af straffeloven
> (Kriminalisering af udtrykkelig billigelse af visse strafbare handlinger som led i religiøs oplæring)[2]
>
> I straffeloven, jf. lovbekendtgørelse nr. 1052 af 4. juli 2016, foretages følgende ændringer:
> I § 136 indsættes som stk. 3:
> »Stk. 3. Den, der som led i religiøs oplæring udtrykkeligt billiger handlinger, som er omfattet af denne lovs §§ 114–114 j, 208, 210, 216, 222, 223, 225, jf. §§ 216, 222 og 223, §§ 237, 244–246, 260 og 261, straffes med bøde eller fængsel indtil 3 år.«

In the draft and preparatory remarks for the Bill the drafting jurists at the Ministry of Justice argue that there have been examples of publishers of religious matter in Denmark who seek to undermine Danish laws and values and support parallel beliefs. Such matters include statements containing support for, for example, the stoning of women or corporal punishment of children, but the remarks do not cite concrete examples or case law to support them.

The Criminal Code already contains a number of provisions that criminalise statements in various forms. One is Article 266 (b) on the dissemination of threats and racism, and Articles 267 and 270 are on defamatory and derogatory statements. In addition, the Criminal Code also makes it possible to punish a person who, by encouragement, advice or deed, has abetted a criminal offence. However, it is a prerequisite to penalising someone for complicity, for example by encouraging the deed, that a specific criminal offence has been committed and that the intention of the person in question has thus to a certain extent been made flesh. Finally, the Criminal Code, in addition to the general rule on participation, contains a number of explicit prohibitions on encouraging or recruiting people to commit offences, etc. Examples are the Article on public incitement to crime, together with Article 114(c) on recruitment for terrorism, and Article 114(e) on promoting a terrorist organisation, and so on. It is thus

2 Forslag til Lov om ændring af straffeloven (Kriminalisering af udtrykkelig billigelse af visse strafbare handlinger som led i religiøs oplæring), som fremsat 5. oktober 2016, https://www.retsinformation.dk/pdfPrint.aspx?id=184011, accessed 1 February 2020.

legal under current law to express support for or approve, for example, the stoning of women or corporal punishment of children, provided that the person in question does not thereby publicly encourage crime, cf. Article 136 of the Criminal Code or abet a specific criminal offence, cf. section 23 of the Criminal Code.

However, this Bill and the new Article 136, section 3, apply expressly to religious education alone and not to other forms of education or influence. The Bill is understood as a tightening of the criminal law regarding religious preachers who, in the logic of the Bill, are seen to have special authority over their congregations, especially children in situations where they might be impressionable. Religious preachers and others who provide religious education thus speak from a general point of view with particular insight and authority in relation to people who must be considered to be particularly vulnerable to their influence when they, for example, seek to and participate in a community of religious action and/or seek religious guidance. Therefore, the legislative logic is that it is particularly problematic if these individuals, through their behaviour, counteract and undermine Danish values by condoning certain criminal offences.

In the draft of and preparatory remarks for the Bill the Ministry's drafting jurists follow the political mandate and state the purpose of the amendment, which is to:

> counteract behaviours that undermine Danish laws and values and support parallel legal beliefs by criminalising the explicit denial of the existence of certain criminal acts as part of religious instruction. The Bill thus safeguards public order and can therefore be implemented within the framework of Article 67 of the Constitution.[3]

The Bill goes on to list examples of cases it is intended to cover, which include the following, all of which are listed without reference to concrete examples or case law:

> Som eksempler på tilfælde, der med lovforslaget tilsigtes omfattet af kriminaliseringen, kan nævnes følgende:
> – En religiøs forkynder eller en anden person udtaler som led i en religiøs oplæring i en "søndagsskole", at det er i orden at slå sine børn som led i opdragelsen.

3 3.2.1, p. 7, Forslag til Lov om ændring af straffeloven (Kriminalisering af udtrykkelig billigelse af visse strafbare handlinger som led i religiøs oplæring), som fremsat 5. oktober 2016, https://www.retsinformation.dk/pdfPrint.aspx?id=184011, accessed 1 February 2020.

- En religiøs forkynder skriver en kronik i et religiøst blad, der bl.a. sendes til menigheden, hvori der argumenteres for, at det kun er naturligt og dermed acceptabelt at gifte sig flere gange (og således begå bigami).
- En religiøs forkynder udtaler under en "gudstjeneste" eller under en fortrolig samtale med en person, der har søgt religiøs vejledning, at det er acceptabelt, at man tiltvinger sig samleje med sin kone.
- En religiøs forkynder laver en række opslag på Facebook i en religiøs Facebook-gruppe, dvs. en gruppe der efter sit indhold primært henvender sig til følgere af den pågældende religion. Opslagene indeholder forskellige billeder af situationer med stening eller halshugninger ledsaget af understøttende citater fra religiøse tekster om samme emne.
- En religiøs forkynder skriver i en kronik, at det står i de religiøse skrifter, at kvinder bør stenes, og forkynderen skriver, at det mener han/hun også. I en efterfølgende religiøs læringssituation spørges forkynderen til sine udtalelser i kronikken. Forkynderen bekræfter—som led i den religiøse oplæring—sit billigende syn på stening af kvinder.[4]

Such scenarios seem to be a figment of politically motivated legal imagination in the Ministry. The examples include the case of a religious preacher or another person who, as part of religious training in a 'Sunday School,' says that it is acceptable for him to beat his children as part of their upbringing; that of a religious preacher who writes an editorial opinion in a religious magazine circulated in his congregation, arguing that it is only natural and thus acceptable to have more than one wife and thus commit the criminal offence of polygamy; that of a religious preacher who states during a sermon or a confidential conversation with a person who has sought religious guidance that it is acceptable to force intercourse on his wife; and that of a religious preacher who makes a number of posts on a religious Facebook group, that is, a group the content of which is primarily aimed at followers of that particular religion. The references contain various imagery of stoning or decapitation accompanied by supporting quotations from religious texts on the same subject. The final example discusses a religious preacher who writes in an editorial opinion that, according to religious writings, women should be stoned for adultery and that he thinks so too, and confirms this subsequently as part of religious education.

This Bill was met with remarkable criticism, amongst others by the Danish Institute for Human Rights, which holds the express mandate to promote and

4 Ibid., p. 14.

protect human rights and equal treatment in Denmark. In criticising the Bill, the Institute highlights that the potential reach and wide application across religious communities of this amendment requires a better assessment of the proportionality of the criminalisation, and questions whether enough has been done to protect the two fundamental freedoms of speech and religion. Further, it finds that the Bill increases the risk of justice becoming arbitrary in the targeting of religious preachers and that the evidence to support its enactment is very weak. Finally, it finds that the limitations on religion and speech are discriminatory and that the arguments for holding that such discrimination is 'factual and proportionate' are not strong enough.[5]

The Council of the Danish Bar and Law Society was also critical of the Bill and recommended not presenting it to parliament. It noted that the Bill criminalises speech in private and that such a legislative limitation of liberties is 'remarkable' by comparison to other limitations. It notes that it would make even a priest in confession criminally liable. It finds that the 'estimates' and political arguments are not 'weighty enough reasons' and that such limitations to freedom of speech and religion require 'significant documentation in arguing that this measure is both proportionate and necessary in a democracy.' By highlighting this it points exactly to the fact that this Bill is politically motivated and that there is little evidence or case law to support it.

Justitia, an independent legal think tank headed by Jacob Mchangama, calls the Bill 'superficial and inadequate,' and says that it risks violating the legal quality criteria of the ECHR and that justice risks becoming 'unpredictable' and 'arbitrary' (Mchangama 2016). Mchangama further highlights the problem caused by the Ministry of Justice not putting forward any evidence of ECtHR precedent, or a single court case that would support such a Bill. He recommends that the Bill not come before the parliament.

Retspolitisk Forening (the Judicial Policy Association) is perhaps most vociferous in its criticism of the basis and proportionality of and need for the Bill. In addition to most of the points of criticism discussed, which it also puts forward, *Retspolitisk Forening* argues:

> [It is] doubtful whether the Ministry's considerations are sound. It must be assumed that the interpretation of the Qur'an, which appears in the television broadcast mentioned above [Mosques documentary], has been

5 Dansk Institut for Menneskerettigheder 2016, "Høring over udkast til lovforslag om ændring af straffeloven," dok. nr. 16/02064-4, https://menneskeret.dk/sites/menneskeret.dk/files/08_august_16/hoeringssvar_til_udkast_til_lovforslag_om_aendring_af_straffel_.pdf, accessed 1 February 2020.

> used for several years. Therefore, if evidence could have been obtained that such preaching was contrary to the law of morality or public order, intervention should have taken place long ago, if in fact it was deemed necessary [in accordance with the ECHR's Article 10(2)]. And such necessity has at least to be probable. Now this Bill is predicated upon the sole basis of a single piece of evidence, which would then constitute necessity [in ECHR, Article 10(2)]. It remains the opinion of *Retspolitisk Forening* that it is greatly exaggerated to claim that the content of the said TV broadcast constitutes a threat to or a violation of morality or public order.[6]

Even *Trykkefrihedsselskabet* (the Society of the Freedom of Press), which is highly critical of much of Islam and sympathetic to the political reasoning, argues against the Bill and calls limiting freedom of religion 'the wrong means to the end' (Fog 2016). It argues that "[i]t is fundamental to the preservation of a free and open democracy that freedom of speech is absolute with only the few natural limitations contained in libel laws and the prohibition against agitation or threatening violence." Additionally, it argues that the Bill would be ineffective and impossible to apply in practice.

In arguing for the Bill in response to the hearing process, the drafting jurists at the Ministry of Justice restated the legal basis for the Bill and argued against amending or changing it. They argued that while freedom of religion is protected in Article 67 of the Constitution, this freedom is limited by the fact that nothing is taught or done that is contrary to morality or public order. In being limited this freedom is subject to the restriction that worship must not include that something is done or taught that is contrary to morality or public order. And thus the Ministry argues that "it is assumed that the legislative power is left with a wide discretion to determine the boundaries arising from considerations of morality or public order."

Ultimately, according to the Ministry's arguments, in limiting religious freedom it is left to legislators to 'assess' using their 'wide discretion' what morality and public order mean, despite the lack of documentation and evidence that it is proportionate and necessary to do so. It further persist in limiting both religious freedom and freedom of speech despite there being little factual evidence, no case law, a poor assessment of proportionality, a lack of weighty and

6 *Retspolitisk Forening*, "Høringssvar ad Forslag til Lov om ændring af straffeloven (Kriminalisering af udtrykkelig billigelse af visse strafbare handlinger som led i religiøs oplæring)," http://www.retspolitik.dk/wp-content/uploads/2014/01/H%C3%B8ringssvar-ad-Forslag-til-Lov-om-%C3%A6ndring-af-straffeloven-religi%C3%B8s-opl%C3%A6ring-.docx, accessed 1 February 2020.

important reasons and no evidence to support the effect of such limitation. The amendment to the Criminal Code became law on 13 December 2016.

14.2 Illegal Coercion

Prior to the passing of the Bill just discussed, a large number of issues were already included in the Criminal Code. Below are quoted the instructions of the Director of Public Prosecutions (*Rigsadvokaten*) to the public prosecutors across Denmark as regards illegal coercion, in accordance with Article 260 of the Criminal Code.

> Bekendtgørelse af straffeloven (LBK nr 976 af 17/09/2019 Gældende)[7]
> [...]
>
> Forbrydelser mod den personlige frihed
> § 260. Med bøde eller fængsel indtil 2 år straffes for ulovlig tvang den, som
> 1) ved vold eller ved trussel om vold, om betydelig skade på gods, om frihedsberøvelse eller om at fremsætte usand sigtelse for strafbart eller ærerørigt forhold eller at åbenbare privatlivet tilhørende forhold tvinger nogen til at gøre, tåle eller undlade noget,
> 2) ved trussel om at anmelde eller åbenbare et strafbart forhold eller om at fremsætte sande ærerørige beskyldninger tvinger nogen til at gøre, tåle eller undlade noget, for så vidt fremtvingelsen ikke kan anses tilbørlig begrundet ved det forhold, som truslen angår.
> Stk. 2. Tvinges nogen til at indgå ægteskab eller til en religiøs vielse uden borgelig gyldighed, kan straffen stige til fængsel indtil 4 år.
> Stk. 3. Tvinges nogen til at bære en beklædningsgenstand, der skjuler vedkommendes ansigt, kan straffen stige til fængsel indtil 4 år.

The instructions are a circular letter and as such a proper legal document, which refers to 're-education trips' (Article 260, section 1),[8] forced marriages (Article 260, section 2) and face covering (Article 260, section 3). In listing these, the instructions argue for the reasoning behind the legislation and its regulatory purpose.

7 https://www.retsinformation.dk/Forms/R0710.aspx?id=209398, accessed 1 November 2019.
8 The Immigration Act further explains the specific rules for re-education travel in sections 17(2), and 44 c.

Rigsadvokatmeddelelsen, afsnittet: Ulovlig tvang (§ 260), (CIRIH nr 10582 af 28/11/2014)[9]

4.1. Genopdragelsesrejser
Straffelovens § 260, stk. 1, om ulovlig tvang kan efter omstændighederne finde anvendelse i forbindelse med såkaldte genopdragelsesrejser, f.eks. i situationer, hvor en person ved vold eller trussel om vold er blevet tvunget til at tage ophold i et andet land.

4.2. Tvangsægteskaber (§ 260, stk. 2)
Straffelovens § 260, stk. 2, har en skærpet strafferamme på indtil 4 års fængsel for ulovlig tvang i forbindelse med indgåelse af ægteskab. Den skærpede sidestrafferamme finder tilsvarende anvendelse, hvis nogen ved ulovlig tvang tvinges til at indgå registreret partnerskab, jf. § 3, stk. 2, i lov om registreret partnerskab.
Forhøjelsen af strafferammen har til formål at afspejle samfundets stærke afstandtagen fra tvangsægteskaber, og at strafpåstanden ved tvang til indgåelse af ægteskab bør afspejle denne forbrydelses grovhed og særligt indgribende betydning for ofret, idet der er tale om, at ofret tvinges til at påtage sig en i princippet livslang forpligtelse af en dybt personlig karakter.
[...]
Formålet er at ligestille sådanne religiøse vielser med tvangsægteskaber i straffelovens forstand, idet mange kvinder er blevet tvunget ind og fastholdt i et ægteskabslignende parforhold baseret på en religiøs vielse. Et eksempel herpå er de såkaldte “nikah-forhold”, som er den mest almindelige betegnelse for et ægteskab i islam, men som er en religiøs vielse uden borgerlig gyldighed.
Der henvises til forarbejderne til lov nr. 434 af 1. maj 2013 (L 143 af 6. februar 2013, de almindelige bemærkninger, pkt. 1 og pkt. 2.2.).
Der kan efter omstændighederne straffes for ulovlig tvang i sammenstød med bl.a. straffelovens § 266 og §§ 245 og 246.

4.3. Beklædningsgenstande (§ 260, stk. 3)
Straffelovens § 260, stk. 3, har en skærpet strafferamme på indtil 4 års fængsel for ulovlig tvang i tilfælde, hvor nogen tvinges til at bære en beklædningsgenstand, der skjuler vedkommendes ansigt.

9 https://www.retsinformation.dk/Forms/R0710.aspx?id=200139, accessed 1 November 2019.

Formålet med forhøjelsen af strafferammen er at afspejle, at denne særlige form for ulovlig tvang indebærer et alvorligt indgreb i den personlige frihed, der vil kunne have væsentlige og vidtrækkende konsekvenser for den pågældende. Som eksempler på beklædningsgenstande, der skjuler vedkommendes ansigt, kan nævnes burka, niqab og anden lignende beklædning.

In her 2018 dissertation on *Honour related crimes*, jurist and researcher Sabba Mirza argues that the recent legislation on these and related crimes is 'imprecise and ineffective' and even 'sloppy legislation' (Mirza 2018; Matzon 2018). Her dissertation is in two parts; the first is a legal analysis and the second is sociolegal. In the combination of these two perspectives she finds that the legislation is unclear, too loosely defined and difficult to apply in a court of law. In an interview she notes that, despite significant criticism, as with other similar legislation, the amendments and changes were enacted into law. She goes as far as to call it a 'moral crusade' caused by an intangible 'moral panic' in society that politicians are struggling to cope with (Matzon 2018).

14.3 Hate Crimes

Article 266B of the Danish Criminal Code is commonly referred to as the racism Article or even the discrimination Article. It states that any person who, publicly or with the intention that it should be more widely disseminated, makes a statement or imparts other information by reason of which a group of people are threatened, insulted or degraded on account of their race, colour, national or ethnic origin, religion, or sexual inclination shall be liable to a fine or to imprisonment.

Bekendtgørelse af straffeloven (LBK nr 976 af 17/09/2019 Gældende)[10]
[…]

§ 266. Den, som på en måde, der er egnet til hos nogen at fremkalde alvorlig frygt for eget eller andres liv, helbred eller velfærd, truer med at foretage en strafbar handling, straffes med bøde eller fængsel indtil 2 år.

10 https://www.retsinformation.dk/Forms/R0710.aspx?id=209398, accessed 1 November 2019.

§ 266 a. Med bøde eller fængsel indtil 1 år straffes den, der, uden at forholdet omfattes af §§ 136 og 266, offentligt fremsætter udtalelser, der tilstræber at fremkalde voldshandlinger eller hærværk.

§ 266 b. Den, der offentligt eller med forsæt til udbredelse i en videre kreds fremsætter udtalelse eller anden meddelelse, ved hvilken en gruppe af personer trues, forhånes eller nedværdiges på grund af sin race, hudfarve, nationale eller etniske oprindelse, tro eller seksuelle orientering, straffes med bøde eller fængsel indtil 2 år.
Stk. 2. Ved straffens udmåling skal det betragtes som en særligt skærpende omstændighed, at forholdet har karakter af propagandavirksomhed.

As with illegal coercion, the Director of Public Prosecutions has published detailed instructions on how to understand and prosecute hate crimes. Whereas these are phrased in language that is much broader than Article 260, section 3, on face covering, it is nevertheless still very possible to identify their relevance to Islam and Muslims. This Article on hate crimes highlights the role and responsibility of the police, what they must demonstrate in order to prosecute, and what kinds of cases have been found to be in violation of Article 266. Some examples are drawn from case law, and here two sections have been chosen for their clear relevance to Islam and Muslims. These are 'expressions that imply that the group is generally of lesser worth as humans' and 'generalising allegations about serious crime.' In the first category is an example of a court ruling where the hate was expressed like this: "the only difference between Mohammedans and rats is that rats don't collect benefits." In the other category there is another example stating, "especially Muslims, who commit violence, crime and rape." Other cases are listed according to criteria of gravity.

Rigsadvokatmeddelelsen, afsnittet: Hadforbrydelser (CIRIH nr 10507 af 30/03/2016)[11]

1. Overblik og tjekliste
Strafbare forhold, der har baggrund i ofrets race, hudfarve, nationale eller etniske oprindelse, tro eller seksuelle orientering, kan være en overtrædelse af:
- Straffelovens § 266 b (se pkt. 2.1., 4.1 og 4.2)
- Lov om forbud mod forskelsbehandling på grund af race mv. (se pkt. 2.2 og 4.5.)

11 https://www.retsinformation.dk/Forms/R0710.aspx?id=199810, accessed 1 November 2019.

Det kan også være relevant at anvende:
- Straffelovens § 81, nr. 6, om strafskærpelse (se pkt. 2.3, 3.2 og 4.6)

1.1. Sager om straffelovens § 266 b
Politiet skal navnlig være opmærksom på følgende:
- Fastlægge indholdet af udtalelsen/meddelelsen. Se pkt. 2.1.1.
- Formål er at afdække, om udtalelsen er af en sådan grovhed, at den er omfattet af § 266 b. Se pkt. 4.1.4.
- Fastlægge hvor, hvordan (f.eks. mundtligt på gaden eller i en blog på internettet) og over for hvem udtalelsen/meddelelsen er fremsat. Se pkt. 2.1.1.
- Formål er at afdække, om udtalelsen er fremsat offentligt eller med forsæt til udbredelse i en videre kreds. Se pkt. 4.1.1.
- Fastlægge baggrunden for udtalelsen/meddelelsen. Se pkt. 2.1.1.
- Formål er at afdække, om gerningsmanden havde forsæt til at true, forhåne eller nedværdige en gruppe af personer på grund af race, hudfarve, nationale eller etniske oprindelse, tro eller seksuelle orientering. Se pkt. 4.1.3.

2.2. Sager om lov om forbud mod forskelsbehandling på grund af race mv.
I sager om lov om forbud mod forskelsbehandling på grund af race, hudfarve, national eller etnisk oprindelse, tro eller seksuelle orientering skal politiet gennem efterforskningen navnlig søge at klarlægge:
- Hvad blev der sagt/udtrykt i forbindelse med, at betjening eller adgang blev nægtet?
- Formålet er at afdække, hvilken begrundelse der blev givet for den pågældende forskelsbehandling (f.eks. dresscode, medlemskab eller alder).
- Hvordan var forholdene på diskoteket, restauranten mv. på det tidspunkt, hvor personen blev nægtet betjening eller adgang? Stemmer forholdene på stedet (f.eks. andre gæsters påklædning eller alder) overens med begrundelsen for at afvise personen?
- Formålet er at undersøge, om forskelsbehandlingen kan være udtryk for diskrimination på grund af race, hudfarve, tro, seksuel orientering mv.

4.1.4. "Trues, forhånes eller nedværdiges" (grovhedskriteriet)
Udtalelsen eller meddelelsen skal have karakter af en trussel, forhånelse eller nedværdigelse (grovhedskriteriet). Dette indebærer, at visse udtalelser mv. falder uden for det strafbare område.

På baggrund af forarbejderne til bestemmelsen, kan der opstilles følgende generelle indskrænkninger i det strafbare område:

- Forhold af mindre grovhed.
- Videnskabeligt fremsatte teorier om racemæssige, nationale eller etniske forskelligheder.
- Udtalelser, der ikke falder i egentlig videnskabelig sammenhæng, men på anden måde som led i en saglig debat.

Se forarbejderne til straffelovens § 266 b (FT 1970–1971, Tillæg A, sp. 1187–1188 og betænkæning nr. 553/1969, s. 34).

Disse indskrænkninger i anvendelsesområdet har til formål at sikre, at der ved anvendelsen af straffelovens § 266 b tages fornødent hensyn til ytringsfriheden. Hensynet til ytringsfriheden blev yderligere understreget ved, at udtrykket "gøres til genstand for nedsættende omtale" i det oprindelige forslag til formulering af § 266 b under Folketingets behandling af lovforslaget blev ændret til "nedværdiges" (FT 1970–1971, Tillæg B, sp. 3001).

Strafbarheden beror på en generel vurdering af, om de relevante udsagn i den konkrete sammenhæng kan anses for egnede til at fremkalde frygt (trusler) eller virke forhånende og/eller nedværdigende. Strafbarheden afhænger ikke af, om den pågældende gruppe rent faktisk har følt sig truet, forhånet eller nedværdiget.

Udtryk, der indebærer, at gruppen generelt mangler værdi som mennesker

Det følger af retspraksis, at udtalelser, der indebærer, at en bestemt gruppe generelt mangler værdi som mennesker, som udgangspunkt opfylder grovhedskriteriet i straffelovens § 266 b. Det gælder f.eks. ved negativt ladede sammenligninger med dyr.

Som eksempler på domme om sammenligninger med dyr, hvor grovhedskriteriet blev anset for opfyldt, kan bl.a. nævnes følgende afgørelser:

- Dom 1.1.6. ("yngler som rotter")
- Dom 1.1.11. ("formere sig som rotter")
- Dom 1.1.12. ("perker svin, sorte so, sorte svin")
- Dom 1.1.16. ("den eneste forskel på muhamedanere og rotter er, at rotter ikke får socialhjælp")
- Dom 1.1.24. ("du ligner en abe", "det er meget værre, at du er fra Marokko—I er en flok aber" mv.)
- Dom 1.1.31. ("alle sorte skal ud af landet", "sorte svin", "abe", "tag ned og spis bananer i palmetræerne"

Herudover er der i en række sager sket domfældelse ved sammenligninger med sygdomme. Som eksempler herpå kan henvises til følgende afgørelser:

- U 1999.296V ("De sorte breder sig alle steder. Det er ligesom en kræftsygdom!")
- U 1995.887H (jøder betegnet som en pest)

Generaliserende påstande om grov kriminalitet

Generaliserende påstande om grov kriminalitet er efter retspraksis som udgangspunkt tilstrækkeligt til, at grovhedskriteriet må anses for opfyldt. Som eksempler på domfældelser i anledning af beskyldninger om grov kriminalitet kan henvises til følgende afgørelser:

- Dom nr. 1.1.5. ("unge indvandrere voldtager og voldtager")
- Dom 1.1.7. ("nej til flere muhammedaner-voldtægter")
- Dom 1.1.9. ("massevoldtægter, grov vold, bandekriminalitet")
- Dom 1.2.1. ("kun er her for at indsmigre sig, indtil de er stærke nok til at henrette os")
- Dom 1.2.7. ("især muslimerne, der laver vold, kriminalitet og begår voldtægt")

Eksempel på frifindelse:

- U 1980.465Ø ("fremmedarbejderne misbruger vort socialsystem")

Andre tilfælde

Af andre eksempler på sager, hvor grovhedskriteriet er anset for opfyldt, kan bl.a. nævnes følgende afgørelser:

- Dom 1.1.2. (hvor tiltalte som tilskuer til en fodboldkamp gentagne gange råbte: "Dem, der hader negere, klapper nu" og klappede)
- Dom 1.2.6. (hvor det blev anset for strafbart til en kvinde i børnenes påhør at udtale: "Sig til dit perkerafkom, at de skal lade være med at glo på mig")

CHAPTER 15

Family Law

Family law and religion are closely connected, both historically and legally. With the growing power of the state since the Reformation, when Denmark became Protestant rather than Catholic, marriage has increasingly become a state institution for governing the family unit. In their chapter on family law, Vinding & Christoffersen 2012 argue that "… the state claims the de facto jurisdiction to define marriage not as a religious institution, but as a publicly-recognised status equally available for all to enter into it and to dissolve accordingly" (Vinding & Christoffersen 2012, 124). This status of being governed and defined by law was seen very clearly in 2012 when Parliament decided to allow same-sex marriage and in effect expected the bishops of the Church of Denmark to produce a gender-neutral ceremony for marriage rituals taking place in church. Besides heated discussions about Church and state relations in Denmark, the question left little doubt about the fact that the state guarantees the legal validity of marriage (Christoffersen & Vinding 2013).

15.1 Marriage and Divorce

The state defines what it means to be married, and marriage is governed mainly by the Marriage Act of 1970 (with later amendments), which not only defines civil marriage and marriage in the Church of Denmark, but also allows for the authorisation of individual preachers from religious communities to perform valid civilly legal marriages. Such authorisation requires recognition by the Ministry of Ecclesiastical Affairs after review by the Advisory Committee on Religious Denominations. The *Act on Religious Communities outside the Church of Denmark*, cited above, in its section 15 specifically considers the issue of whether a guardian's approval is a requirement or merely a ceremonial part of the marriage.

An important part of what qualifies an individual preacher to perform marriages with civil legal validity is that he or she meets the requirements of decorum and attends a mandatory course on Danish family law, liberty and democracy.

Lov om ændring af lov om ægteskabs indgåelse og opløsning (Decorumkrav og obligatorisk kursus i dansk familieret, frihed og folkestyre) (LOV nr 1729 af 27/12/2016)[1]

I lov om ægteskabs indgåelse og opløsning, jf. lovbekendtgørelse nr. 1818 af 23. december 2015, foretages følgende ændring:
1. I *§ 16* indsættes som *stk. 3–8:*
Stk. 3. Som udøver af offentlig myndighed skal en præst i et trossamfund som nævnt i stk. 1, nr. 2 og 3, udvise en adfærd, der ikke gør den pågældende uegnet eller uværdig til at udøve offentlig myndighed.
Stk. 4. Der kan ske tilbagekaldelse af en vielsesbemyndigelse til en præst i et trossamfund som nævnt i stk. 1, nr. 2 og 3, hvis den pågældende præst ikke længere opfylder betingelserne for tildeling af vielsesbemyndigelse.
Stk. 5. Tildeling af vielsesbemyndigelse skal betinges af, at præsten i et trossamfund som nævnt i stk. 1, nr. 2 og 3, inden 6 måneder efter meddelelse af vielsesbemyndigelse gennemfører et kursus i dansk familieret, frihed og folkestyre. Fristen på 6 måneder kan efter ansøgning forlænges ved lovligt forfald. Kirkeministeriet kan fritage præsten for at deltage i kurset, hvis præsten har et tilsvarende dokumenteret kendskab til dansk familieret, frihed og folkestyre. Præsten skal fremlægge dokumentation herfor.
Stk. 6. Som afslutning på kurset, jf. stk. 5, udleveres et kursusbevis, ligesom præsten skal underskrive en løfteerklæring om, at den pågældende vil overholde dansk lovgivning.

The comments on the draft note on the question of decorum that what breaches decorum must be based on an assessment in each individual case. Thus, it is impossible to provide an exhaustive list of the situations that may lead to a problem with decorum. However, the comments provide examples of what might lead to trial in court. Decorum would be in question if the religious preacher were to marry a minor without the permission of the civil authorities or to perform a marriage without the consent of both parties. This was later changed to make any marriage by a person under the age of 18 illegal. In addition, failure to participate in the mandatory course in Danish family law, liberty and democracy might lead to the marriage authorisation being revoked. Similarly, a more serious criminal offence may also lead to revocation.[2]

1 https://www.retsinformation.dk/Forms/R0710.aspx?id=185820, accessed 1 November 2019.
2 "Bemærkninger til lovforslaget," Lovforslag L 30, Folketinget 2016–2017, 5 October 2016, p. 13,

15.2 Children

There is very little legal regulation and very few texts that deal with the question of Muslim children or Islamic views on children. As mentioned above, it is an offence to minors or to strike them, but this is general.

However, one minor mention relevant to the religious communities outside the Church of Denmark is that only people who are baptised and confirmed may be godparents as witnesses to the baptism. It is a minor issue, but it demonstrates the reach of the state in regulating the Church that this is regulated by a decree from the Ministry of Ecclesiastical Affairs.

Anordning om dåb i Folkekirken (Dåbsanordning) (AND nr 1 af 02/01/2008)[3]

§ 6. Ved barnedåb skal der være mindst to og højst fem faddere ud over forældrene til barnet. Ved dåben skal mindst to faddere være til stede som vidner.
Stk. 2. Ved dåb af en voksen skal mindst to vidner være til stede.
Stk. 3. Fadderne (vidnerne) skal være døbt med den kristne dåb. De må ikke have tilsluttet sig et ikke-kristent trossamfund. Fadderne skal være konfirmeret eller have nået konfirmationsalderen.

15.3 Mediation

A surprising part of Danish law is the executive order on ecclesiastical mediation in cases of separation and divorce, which follows from section 40 of the Marriage Act, which states that mediation is an option available to the parties. This option lingers on from earlier times, where in certain situations mediation or attempted mediation was mandatory before divorce proceedings could be initiated. Currently, the order makes it possible for a priest to mediate between and seek to reconcile the parties before divorce. It rests on the premise that both parties want such mediation and requires the Church of Denmark to provide such services. However, the surprising part comes with section 3, which states that if the couple or one of them belongs to a religious community out-

---

https://www.ft.dk/ripdf/samling/20161/lovforslag/l30/20161_l30_som_fremsat.pdf, accessed 1 February 2020.

3 https://www.retsinformation.dk/Forms/R0710.aspx?id=114174, accessed 1 February 2020.

side the Church of Denmark, the 'priest' of the community may attempt mediation. Echoing the discussions above and in other legislation about Islamic councils, TV documentaries that seek to expose imams and assumptions about parallel legal orders, it seems that allowing for religious mediation is sanctioned by law. Worth noting, too, is the fact that this executive order is signed by the same minister who set much of the politically motivation legislation in motion.

Bekendtgørelse om kirkelig mægling i sager om separation og skilsmisse[4]

I medfør af § 40 i lov om ægteskabs indgåelse og opløsning, jf. lovbekendtgørelse nr. 1096 af 7. oktober 2014, og efter forhandling med social- og indenrigsministeren fastsættes:

§ 1. Inden der gives separation eller skilsmisse, kan der, hvis begge parter ønsker det, ske mægling ved en præst.

§ 2. Er ægtefællerne medlemmer af folkekirken, sker mægling ved præsten i det sogn, hvor ægtefællerne eller en af dem bor eller opholder sig.

Stk. 2. Tilhører ægtefællerne eller en af dem en anden folkekirkelig menighed end sognemenigheden, kan mægling dog foretages af præsten for denne anden menighed.

Stk. 3. En præst i folkekirken kan undlade mægling, hvis præsten ikke ville have været forpligtet til at vie ægtefællerne.

§ 3. Tilhører ægtefællerne eller en af dem et trossamfund uden for folkekirken, kan mægling foretages af præsten for den menighed, som ægtefællerne eller en af dem tilhører.

§ 4. Bekendtgørelsen træder i kraft den 1. december 2015.

Stk. 2. Bekendtgørelse nr. 16 af 15. januar 1990 om mægling i sager om separation og skilsmisse ophæves.

Kirkeministeriet, den 19. november 2015

Bertel Haarder

---

4 https://www.retsinformation.dk/eli/lta/2015/1303, accessed 1 November 2019.

CHAPTER 16

Concluding Remarks

The objective of this volume was to present the legal status of Islam in Denmark based on the documents that may give insight to this. This makes legislation and regulation on Islam, Islamic religious communities and Muslims the specific case and topic for this volume, but not necessarily a special case in Danish regulation.

As discussed and presented throughout there is in Denmark a general regulatory paradigm of religion, which seeks to balance the legitimate role and place of religion in the public sphere. The evidence of such a general regulatory paradigm appears in existing legislation as a general respect for religion in Denmark as well as in a regulatory framework that limits religious autonomy within public law. Here, of course, the Church of Denmark is of great importance, and much public discourse and legislation concern this particular institution as the primary special case in law on religion. In many cases, this majority position heavily influences the status of Islam and Muslims. Rights, freedoms and permissions, as well as limitions and controls that work on Islamic communities are directly or indirectly related to the general status of religion, as well as from the significane of the Church of Denmark. Because much of the public and legislative discourse on religion is so closely related to the Church of Denmark as the primary case, the developing cross-disciplinary study of Law and Religion owes much to Ecclesiastical Law, although this field of study in law has not been very vibrant in recent years.

Second to the general framework is the specific case of regulating Islam and Islamic communities in the context and relationship with the Church of Denmark, as well as state, society and culture. Here, there seems to be a binary of enabling and disabling trends in particular in recent legislation. As an urgent topic in the legislative agenda from 2016 and onwards, Islam, Islamic communities and ideas peceived to be related to certain iterations of Islam were seen as something to curtail. However, while this view on Islam was evident in much of the political motivation and in the guidelines of various drafting remarks, the provisions and regulations were phrased generally and not explicitly to limit certain Islamic communites.

The legal documents presented and dicussed in this volume relating to this question of general legitimacy of religion are frequent, in cases such as the regulation of the religious communities outside the Church of Denmark, the limitations from article 70 of the constitution, as well as in the many examples of demands for decorum and public order across legal documents. However, some of the particular acts and bills that sought to disable certain Islamic communities and groups were generally applicable, and so the legislative move to disable particular groups had the impact of deligitimising religion more generally. This was the case of the criminalising of the explicit approval of certain crimes, the case of limitations on what may be taught and preached, as well as limits for support of religious ethos organisations in the *Public Education Act*. These all seem like blunt instruments that were enacted for a specific, albeit not explicit, political purpose, but generally phrased and thus with significant impact on religion generally.

This recent and often expressly politically motivated legislation may be understood as top-down regulation disabling Islam, specifically, and deligitimising religion, generally. In contrast, much of the general regulatory framework on the permissions and limitations on religion as well as the specific regulations of Islamic communities work to legitimise religion generally and to include and enable Muslims specifically. This is a regulatory logic that works from below, so to speak, drawing on general principles of human rights, non-discrimination and equal treatment. This was the case of the circular letter on co-operation between the police and local Muslim communities, where significant instructions and examples are given on how to work with the communities and include them in the public responsibilies. Also, the case of regulating and supervising chaplains demonstrates how Muslim spiritual care is included in the everyday life of prison inmates, and how reasonable accommodation is provided for access to worship, religious texts, dress, dietary requirements, holidays and more. Explicitly for the religious leaders of recognised communities, this included the extended degree of confidentiality. The last example in this volume provides perhaps the most contrastful case of this kind of buttom-up enabling of religious communities, including Islamic communities. Section 3 of the executive order on ecclesiastical mediation allowed for a divorcing couple to seek the religious or spiritual leader of their community to attempt mediation. For Muslims, this would most likely be an imam from an Islamic community. The notion of an imam having public authority and legitimate occasion to mediate and counsel in such family law cases seems to be in contrast to the governing political sentiments in many of the legal documents discussed here.

The significance of this final example is that it illustrates so clearly how the top-down logic of politically motivated regulation that deligitimises religion and disables Islamic communities runs counter to much of the pragmatic and practical regulation from below that is rooted in both principles and sound jurisprudence. This is not always the case, naturally, but these two approaches seem to be at odds in the legal documents on Islam in Denmark. From above, the political motivation for or even political fictions in certain legislation gave testimony to an understanding of Islam as synomous with parallel legal orders, as anti-democratic and as something to be limited. However, from below, the concluding finding of this volume is that there is convincing evidence of the amicable regulation of religious communities, and Islamic communities and Muslims as our specific cases, in the everyday situations when interacting with state, society and culture as well as in close relation to the regulations of the Church of Denmark.

Bibliography

Advokatrådet. 2016a. "Høring over forslag til lov om ændring af folkeoplysningsloven og ligningsloven (Indsats mod foreninger, som modarbejder eller underminerer demokrati eller grundlæggende friheds- og menneskerettigheder)," 18 August 2016. Unpublished public consultation response.

Advokatrådet, 2016b. "Høring over udkast til lov om ændring af udlændingeloven (Indførelse af en offentlig sanktionsliste over udenlandske religiøse forkyndere m.fl., som kan udelukkes fra at indrejse)," 1 November 2016. Unpublished public consultation response.

Afgørelse om 'Copenhagen Lads'. 2005. Det Rådgivende Udvalg vedr. Trossamfund, (København: Kirkeministeriet, 2005).

Agreement Paper 2016, "Aftale mellem regeringen og Socialdemokraterne, Dansk Folkeparti og Det Konservative Folkeparti om initiativer rettet mod religiøse forkyndere, som søger at undergrave danske love og værdier og understøtte parallelle retsopfattelser", Kirkeministeriet, doknr. 65672/16, 31, May 2016.

Beckford, Jim, 2002. "Banal discrimination: Equality of respect for beliefs and worldviews in the UK," in D. Davis & G. Besier (eds), *International perspectives on freedom and equality of religious belief* (Waco, TX: Dawson Institute of Church-State Studies, 2002).

Bergeaud-Blackler, Florence, Johan Fischer and John Lever (eds). 2015. *Halal matters: Islam, politics and markets in global perspective* (Abingdon: Routledge, 2015).

Betænkning 1544. Folkekirkens styre. 2014. Betænkning fra Udvalget om en mere sammenhængende og moderne styringsstruktur for folkekirken (Copenhagen: Ministry of Ecclesiastical Affairs, 2014).

Betænkning 1564. 2017. En samlet lovregulering om andre trossamfund end folkekirken. (Copenhagen: Ministry of Ecclesiastical Affairs, 2017).

Berlingske, "Udlændinge betaler ufrivillig kirkeskat," 4 May 2009, https://www.berlingske.dk/samfund/udlaendinge-betaler-ufrivillig-kirkeskat, accessed 1 November 2019.

Berlingske, "Magasin tabte tørklæde-sag," 25 February 2003, https://www.berlingske.dk/samfund/magasin-tabte-toerklaede-sag, accessed 1 November 2019.

Bielefeldt, Heiner. 2011. "Report of the Special Rapporteur on freedom of religion or belief,"

(A/HCR/19/60), 22 December, https://www.ohchr.org/Documents/HRBodies/HRCouncil/RegularSession/Session19/A-HRC-19-60_en.pdf, accessed 1 November 2019.

Bielefeldt, Heiner. 2016. "Report of the Special Rapporteur on freedom of religion and belief on his mission to Denmark," (A/HRC/34/50/Add.1), 28 December, https://documents-dds-ny.un.org/doc/UNDOC/GEN/G16/442/36/PDF/G1644236.pdf accessed 1 November 2019.

Bøe, Marianne. 2018. *Annotated Legal documents on Islam in Europe: Norway* (Leiden: Brill, 2018).

Christoffersen, Lisbet. 2010. "State, Church and Religion in Denmark", in Christoffersen, Modéer & Andersen, *Law & Religion in the 21st Century—Nordic Perspectives* (Copenhagen: DJØF Publishing, 2010).

Christoffersen, Lisbet. 2012. "Den aktuelle danske religionsretlige model," in Christoffersen, Iversen, Kærgård & Warburg (eds.), *Fremtidens Danske Religionsmodel* (Copenhagen: Anis, 2012).

Christoffersen, Lisbet. 2016. "Høringssvar vedr. Kulturministeriets forslag til love om ændring af folkeoplysningsloven og ligningsloven (indsats mod foreninger, som modarbejder eller underminerer demokrati eller grundlæggende friheds- og menneskerettigheder)," 11 August, Roskilde University. Unpublished public consultation response.

Christoffersen, Lisbet. 2019a. "Transnational Religious Law: Exemplified by the United Methodist Church," in B. Lemann Kristiansen, K. Mitkidis, L. Munkholm, L. Neumann, & C. Pelaudeix (eds), *Transnationalisation and legal actors: Legitimacy in question* pp. 201–215 (New York: Routledge, 2019).

Christoffersen, Lisbet. 2019b. "Religionsretlig lovgivning 2014–2019: Introduktion til bidrag og temaer i kirkeretsantologi 2019," in Christoffersen, Jørgensen & Andersen (eds), *Religionsretlig lovgivning. Kirkeretsantologi 2019: Trossamfundslov. Blasfemibestemmelse* (Frederiksberg: Eksistensen Akademisk, 2019).

Christoffersen, Lisbet, & Niels Valdemar Vinding. 2013. "Challenged Pragmatism—Conflicts of Law and Religion in the Danish Labour Market," in *International Journal of Discrimination and the Law*, vol. 3, no. 2–3, Sage Publications

Dansk Institut for Menneskerettigheder. 2016a. "Høring over forslag om indsats mod foreninger, som modarbejder eller underminerer demokrati eller grundlæggende friheds- og menneskerettigheder," dok. nr. 16/02068-4, https://menneskeret.dk/sites/menneskeret.dk/files/08_august_16/hoeringssvar_til_forslag_til_lov_om_aendring_af_folkeoplysning_.pdf, accessed 1 February 2020.

Dansk Institut for Menneskerettigheder. 2016b. "Høring over udkast til lovforslag om ændring af straffeloven," dok. nr. 16/02064-4, https://menneskeret.dk/sites/menneskeret.dk/files/08_august_16/hoeringssvar_til_udkast_til_lovforslag_om_aendring_af_straffel_.pdf, accessed 1 February 2020.

Dansk Tyrkisk Islamisk Stiftelse 2016. "Høring vedrørende den nye trossamfundslov." Unpublished public consultation response.

Den Katolske Kirke i Danmark. 2018. "Høringssvar til L80," Unpublished public consultation response.

Det Jødiske Samfund i Danmark. 2017. "Høring over udkast til forslag til Lov om trossamfund uden for folkekirken," Copenhagen, 30 August, Unpublished public consultation response.

"Domme og nævnssager om diskrimination på grund af etnicitet og handicap 2009–2014", Als Research APS, September 2015.

Ekstra Bladet, "Burkaforbud fylder år: Så mange bøder er der givet." 31 July 2019, https://ekstrabladet.dk/112/burkaforbud-fylder-aar-saa-mange-boeder-er-der-givet/7731836, accessed 1 November 2019.

European Commission against Racism and Intolerance, *ECRI Report on Denmark Report from the Fifth Monitoring Cycle*, CRI/2017/20, 16 May 2017

Ferrari, Silvio. 2002. "Islam and the Western European Model of Church and State Relations," in W.A.R. Shadid and P.S. van Koningsveld (eds.), *Religious Freedom and the Neutrality of the State: The Position of Islam in the European Union*. (Leuven: Peeters, 2002).

Fog, Aia. 2016. "TFSs høringssvar om imamloven," https://www.trykkefrihed.dk/blog/1953/tfss-h%C3%B8ringssvar-om-imamloven.htm, accessed 1 February 2020.

Gammeltoft Hansen, Hans. 2006. "§ 4," in Henrik Zahle (ed.), *Danmarks Riges Grundlov med kommentarer* (Copenhagen, Jurist- og Økonomforbundets Forlag, 2006).

Gammeltoft Hansen, Hans, & Pernille Esdahl. 2019. *Lov om trossamfund med kommentarer* (Copenhagen: Jurist- og Økonomforbundets Forlag, 2019).

Jacobsen, Brian Arly. 2014. "Denmark", in J.S. Nielsen et al. (eds.), *Yearbook of Muslims in Europe*, vol. 6, (Leiden: Brill, 2014).

Jacobsen, Brian Arly. 2015. "Hellige bygninger på grænsefladen i dansk kommunalpolitik," *Religionsvidenskabeligt Tidsskrift*, 62 (2015), pp. 91–105.

Jacobsen, Brian Arly, & Niels Valdemar Vinding. 2019. "Denmark" in O. Scharbrodt, et al (eds), *Yearbook on Muslims in Europe*, vol. 10 (Leiden: Brill, 2019).

Kristiansen, Bettina Lemann. 2019. "Ligebehandling som konfliktpunkt i regulering af trossamfundenes forhold," in Lisbet Christoffersen, Anders Jørgensen & Svend Andersen (eds.), *Religionsretlig lovgivning. Kirkeretsantologi 2019: Trossamfundslov. Blasfemibestemmelse* (Copenhagen: Eksistensen Akademisk, 2019).

Laurence, Jonathan. 2012. *The emancipation of Europe's Muslims: The state's role in minority integration* (Princeton, NJ: Princeton University Press, 2012).

Marzouki, N., D. McDonnell & O. Roy. 2016. *Saving the people: How populists hijack religion* (London: Hurst, 2016).

Matzon, Mads. 2018. "Forbud mod æresforbrydelser er lovsjusk," DJØFbladet, 18 April, https://www.djoefbladet.dk/artikler/2018/4/forbud-mod--ae-resforbrydelser-er-lovsjusk.aspx, accessed 1 February 2020.

Mchangama, Jakob. 2016. "Analyse: Lovudkast om kriminalisering af religiøse ytringer er uklart og problematisk i forhold til menneskerettighedskonventionen," http://justitia-int.org/analyse-lovudkast-om-kriminalisering-af-religiose-ytringer-er-uklart-og-problematisk-i-forhold-til-menneskerettighedskonventionen/, accessed 1 February 2020.

Mirza, Kumm Sabba. 2018. *Æresrelaterede Forbrydelser. Strafferetlige perspektiver* (Copenhagen: Jurist- og Økonomforbundets Forlag, 2018).

My Constitutional Act, "My Constitutional Act with Explanations," 9th Edition, The Communications Section, Danish Parliament, August 2012.

Politiken, 26 August 2015, https://politiken.dk/indland/art5586871/Universitet-%C3%A5bner-master-i-islamisk-teologi, accessed 1 November 2019.

"Rapport om brugen af niqab og burka," 2009, https://hum.ku.dk/faknyt/nyheder_fra_2010/2010/brugen-af-niqab-og-burka.pdf, accessed 1 February 2020.

Retspolitisk Forening, "Høringssvar til L48," 1 November 2016.

Retspolitisk Forening, "Høringssvar ad Forslag til Lov om ændring af straffeloven (Kriminalisering af udtrykkelig billigelse af visse strafbare handlinger som led i religiøs oplæring)," http://www.retspolitik.dk/wp-content/uploads/2014/01/H%C3%B8ringssvar-ad-Forslag-til-Lov-om-%C3%A6ndring-af-straffeloven-religi%C3%B8s-opl%C3%A6ring-.docx, accessed 1 February 2020.

Rytter, Jens Elo. 2019. "Demokratiske minimumskrav til trossamfund som betingelse for særrettigheder? Overvejelserne bag Det Rådgivende Udvalgs hidtidige praksis og flertalspositionen i Trossamfundsudvalget," in Lisbet Christoffersen, Anders Jørgensen & Svend Andersen (eds.), *Religionsretlig lovgivning. Kirkeretsantologi 2019: Trossamfundslov. Blasfemibestemmelse* (Copenhagen: Eksistensen Akademisk, 2019).

Stuart, Alison. 2010. "Freedom of Religion and Gender Equality: Inclusive or Exclusive?" in *Human Rights Law Review*, 10 (2010), 429–459.

Stage, Carsten. 2011. *Tegningekrisen som mediebegivenhed og danskhedskamp*. (Aarhus: Aarhus Universitetsforlag, 2011).

Time, "Denmark Bans Kosher and Halal Animal Slaughter," 28 July 2015, http://time.com/3974498/denmark-ban-kosher-halal/, accessed 1 July 2019.

UN Human Rights Committee, *Sixth Periodic report on Denmark under the International Covenant on Civil and Political Rights*, 10 November 2015, CCPR/C/DNK/CO/6

Vejrup Nielsen, M. 2012. "Kirkelig autonomi i de nordiske lande," in Christoffersen, Iversen, Kærgård & Warburg (eds.), *Fremtidens Danske Religionsmodel* (Copenhagen: Anis Publishers, 2012).

Vinding, Niels Valdemar. 2012. "De fra folkekirken afvigende trossamfund" in Christoffersen, Iversen, Kærgård & Warburg (eds.), *Fremtidens Danske Religionsmodel* (Copenhagen: Anis Publishers, 2012).

Vinding, Niels Valdemar. 2013. *Muslim Positions in the Religio-Organisational Fields of Denmark, Germany and England*. Publikationer fra Det Teologiske Fakultet, nr. 42 (Copenhagen: Faculty of Theology, 2013).

Vinding, Niels Valdemar. 2016. "Islamforskning og islamiske studier på Københavns Universitet", *Tidsskrift for Islamforskning* (*TIFO*), 10 (2016): Dansk islamforskning anno 2016, pp. 21–35, https://tifoislam.dk/article/download/24870/21777/.

Vinding, Niels Valdemar. 2019a. "Civilsamfundet og udgrænsningen af de danske trossamfund," in Brian Arly Jacobsen, Henrik Reintoft Christensen & Signe A.E. Larsen (eds.), *Religion i det offentlige rum—et dansk perspektiv* (Aarhus: Aarhus Universitetsforlag, 2019).

Vinding, Niels Valdemar. 2019b. "State and Church in Denmark" in G. Robbers (ed.), *Church and State in the European Union*, 3rd ed. (Bern: Peter Lang Verlag, 2019).

Vinding, Niels Valdemar. 2019c. "Godkendelse og anerkendelse af de islamiske trossamfund i Danmark," in Lisbet Christoffersen, Anders Jørgensen & Svend Andersen (eds.), *Religionsretlig lovgivning. Kirkeretsantologi 2019: Trossamfundslov. Blasfemibestemmelse* (Copenhagen: Eksistensen Akademisk, 2019).

Vinding, Niels Valdemar. 2020. "Discrimination of Muslims in Denmark," in Saral & Bahçecik (eds.), *State, Religion and Muslims: Between Discrimination and Protection at the Legislative, Executive and Judicial Level* (Leiden: Brill, 2020).

Vinding, Niels Valdemar, & Lisbet Christoffersen. 2012. *Danish Regulation of Religion, State of Affairs, and Qualitative Reflections*, Publications from the Faculty of Theology, No. 36, (Copenhagen: University of Copenhagen, 2012).

Zahle, Henrik, & Lund Hansen. 2019. "Rituel slagtning og religionsfrihed," in *EU-ret & Menneskeret 1998*, https://www.djoef-forlag.dk/publications/eumenneskeret/html/artikler/Art1998_2_058.htm, accessed 1 November 2019.

Index

Printed in the United States
By Bookmasters